EURIPIDES

Hecuba

EURIPIDES

Hecuba

Introduction, Translation and Commentary

Robin Mitchell-Boyask
TEMPLE UNIVERSITY

Focus Classical Library
Focus Publishing
R. Pullins Company
Newburyport MA

THE FOCUS CLASSICAL LIBRARY

Series Editors • James Clauss and Stephen Esposito
Hesiod: Theogony • Richard Caldwell • 1987
The Heracles of Euripides • Michael Halleran • 1988
Aristophanes: Lysistrata • Jeffrey Henderson • 1988
Euripides: Medea • Anthony Podlecki • 1991
Aristophanes: Acharnians • Jeffrey Henderson • 1992
Aristophanes: Clouds • Jeffrey Henderson • 1992
The Homeric Hymns • Susan Shelmerdine • 1995
Aristophanes: Acharnians, Lysistrata, Clouds • Jeffrey Henderson • 1997
Euripides: Bacchae • Stephen Esposito • 1998
Terence: Brothers • Charles Mercier • 1998
Sophocles: Antigone • Ruby Blondell • 1998
Euripides: Hippolytus • Michael Halleran • 2000
Aristophanes: The Birds • Jeffrey Henderson • 1999
Sophocles: King Oidipous • Ruby Blondell • 2002
Sophocles: Oidipous at Colonus • Ruby Blondell • 2002
Sophocles: The Theban Plays • Ruby Blondell • 2002
Euripides: Medea, Hippolytus, Heracles, Bacchae • Stephen Esposito, ed. • 2002
Golden Verses: Poetry of the Augustan Age • Paul T. Alessi • 2003
Vergil's Aeneid • Richard Caldwell • 2003
Sophocles: Philoktetes • Seth Schein • 2003
Ovid: Metamorphoses • Z. Philip Ambrose • 2004
Euripides: The Trojan Women • Diskin Clay • 2004

Table of Contents

Introduction

Through accidents of history there are far more extant dramas by Euripides than by the other two great Athenian tragedians of the fifth century B. C. E., Aeschylus and Sophocles.[1] This relative abundance has, strangely, at times worked against his reputation in modernity, as critics simply have had a greater ranger of unselected material to pick apart at leisure and have thus restricted the sort of unstinting praise reserved for Sophocles to the "Big Three" of Euripides: the *Medea*, *Hippolytus*, and *Bacchae*. While few serious students of Euripidean drama would fault any praise for this trio, still, in the modern world, it has only been recently acknowledged that more of the Euripidean corpus might warrant praise if we adopt aesthetic criteria beyond the Sophocles-based model espoused in the *Poetics* of Aristotle, written a full century after dramas such as the *Oedipus Tyrannus*, *Medea*, and, indeed, *Hecuba*.[2] The *Hecuba*, which during the Byzantine and the Renaissance eras was particularly popular, is certainly one tragic drama which benefits from a more open mind about what constitutes an effective exploration of the genre, for few other tragedies leave their audiences with such a sense of utter devastation as does Euripides' enactment of the sufferings of the former queen of Troy and her reaction to them. After all, Aristotle himself acknowledged (*Poetics*, Ch 13), "although Euripides manages badly in other respects, he is obviously the most tragic of poets."[3] Aristotle there further stresses that the impact of the unhappy endings is particularly felt "on stage and in performance," and thus it is perhaps no accident that the *Hecuba* has been held in higher esteem during eras when performance has

---

1 On the survival of manuscripts of Greek drama after their initial performances and through the Renaissance, see Csapo and Slater (1995) 1-38.

2 Michelini (1987) discusses the problems of viewing Euripides through a purely Sophoclean perspective.

3 The translation is by Richard Janko (Hackett. Indianapolis, 1987)

1

been more central to the understanding of drama, eras such as the Renaissance and our own time.[4]

THE PERFORMANCE OF DRAMA IN ATHENS

The original performances of tragic dramas occurred in Athens every spring in the Theater of Dionysus, during a festival held in honor of the same god, before an audience of 15,000-18,000, composed of Athenians and visitors from throughout the Greek world. This was one of the highlights of the Athenian calendar and the city itself virtually ceased normal activities during its duration. The audience was notionally, if not actually, all male, so that, even if women were present, the intended audience was still the men of Athens. While women were generally restricted from public activities, they did have prominent roles in the religious life of the city, and drama was part of a religious festival, so it is possible that women did attend the theater. The Theater of Dionysus itself was a large, open-air venue on the south slope of the Acropolis, overlooked by the Parthenon, occupying a semi-circular bowl, though the all-stone theater visible today there is a Roman reconstruction from the first century C.E. of a form of the theater reworked by Lycourgus around 350 B.C.E.[5] The fifth-century audience sat on stone benches closer to the stage, and on wooden benches higher up, with the crowd perhaps spilling on to the bare slope higher still; the audience was divided into wedges, possibly according to the tribal affiliation that had organized Athens politically earlier in the fifth century, with one tribe per wedge in the semi-circle and the more prominent citizens seated in front.[6] This

---

4   On the popularity of *Hecuba* during the Byzantine and Renaissance eras, see Mossman (1992) 222-43 and Malcolm Heath, "'*Iure Principen Locum Tenet*: Euripides' *Hecuba*," 218-60 in Mossman 2003.

5   On the nature of the Athenian theater, including the evidence in original sources, see Csapo and Slater (1995), especially 79-80, and Wiles (1997).

6   There is some question whether the theater audience was divided into wedges according to tribal affiliation; see Rhodes (2003) 10. In support of the political mapping of the Athenian audience, see several articles in Winkler and Zeitlin (1990): Simon Goldhill's "The Great Dionysia and Civic Ideology" (97-129), on display, dramatic festival, and the ideology of the *polis*; Josiah Ober and Barry Strauss' "Drama, Political Rhetoric and the Discourse of Athenian Democracy" (237-270) on the relationship between the audiences at the Theater of Dionysus and the Pnyx, the meeting place of the Assembly; and John Winkler's "The Ephebe's Song: *Tragoidia* and Polis" (20-62), pages 39-40 specifically on the seating plan, with bibliography.

arrangement mirrored the seating plan of the Athenian Assembly (more on this below). Actors generally stood on a slightly raised stage in front of a wooden building (*skênê*), which was painted as the drama's setting required.[7] Actors could enter the acting area through a door in the *skênê*, or through two long entrance ramps (*eisodoi*); such entrances would thus be visible to the audience before the characters in the acting area. In between the seats and the *skênê* lay the *orchestra*, the circular (or, possibly, square or trapezoidal) area in which the chorus sang and danced, so the chorus formed a literally mediating body in between the audience and the characters. While the actors and chorus had their distinct spaces, no impenetrable barrier separated them, and the actors frequently moved into the orchestra as the action required; it is generally thought now that the area immediately in front of the *skênê* was only slightly, if at all, raised, thus facilitating such movement by the actors.

Every year three poets were granted a chorus by Athens and each presented three tragedies and a satyr play, a comic drama in which the chorus were dressed as satyrs (mythological creatures whose lower halves were goats and upper humans) and which seemed to have poked fun at the more sorrowful events that had preceded it. These three tragic dramas were not, after Aeschylus, normally trilogic, with a single larger myth enacted across all three, but were independently conceived, though one might imagine thematic links intended among them. The three playwrights engaged, so typically Greek, in a competition with one another for prizes awarded by the city of Athens. We do not know on what basis the judges decided the prizes, but one imagines that their decisions could be controversial (one is tempted to compare the annual uproars over our Academy Awards). Euripides, while achieving enough notoriety to be regularly ridiculed by the comic dramas of Aristophanes, only won first prize five times (and one of those posthumously). His *Medea*, so popular in our time, finished third out of three. His relative lack of success, especially compared with Sophocles, might have contributed to his departure from Athens late in his life for the court of the king of Macedon, a traditional story about Euripides that has recently been called into serious question.[8] But even Sophocles' *Oedipus Tyrannus*, considered the greatest Greek tragedy since Aristotle wrote his *Poetics* in the century after its first production, failed to win and instead took second!

---

7 On the *skênê* see Csapo and Slater (1995) 79-80. Wiles, (1997) Chapter 7 discusses the symbolic uses of the *skênê*.

8 See Scullion (2003).

A tragic poet worked inside certain broad, but fixed, parameters. The chorus, during Euripides' career, had fifteen members, whose official leader typically engaged the principal actors more directly than the rest of the collective. The chorus members, who, while amateurs, still had to be highly trained at both singing and dancing and capable of representing slave women, old men and warriors (and sometimes all on the same day), were likely young men, possibly otherwise engaged in their military training; the late John Winkler argued, controversially, that the choral dances resembled the precise corporate movements that typified the maneuvers of hoplite soldiers, who moved in exact conformity with shields linked to form a moving wall.[9] Following the prologue spoken by one or two of the actors, the chorus entered the *orchestra*, the central circle in front of the *skênê* through either of two side entrances (*eisodoi*) at the front of the audience (see diagram). There they remained, with extraordinarily rare exceptions (e.g. Sophocles' *Ajax* and the *Eumenides* of Aeschylus) until the end of the drama, when they typically, but not universally, were the last to leave the acting area; in the *Hecuba* I believe Hecuba herself is left by the chorus alone in the orchestra at the end. The chorus did not serve as the voice of the poet, expressing what "he really thought," but served as a sounding board for the main characters or a filter through which the audience could digest the actions and sentiments expressed by the characters. Above all, in many dramas, the chorus itself served as a character, participating in or rejecting the plans of the protagonists. The chorus thus formed the community against which the actions of the heroic figures behind them were played out. I shall have more to say about the chorus of Euripides' *Hecuba* in the Interpretive Essay at the end of this volume.

In addition to the chorus, each playwright received two or three speaking actors, all of them men, and any number of mute extras. These actors were professionals, and, from the middle of the fifth century, had their own competition and prizes. Greek tragedy likely grew out of choral songs in honor of Dionysus, known as *dithyrambs*, and, at some point in the sixth century, a single chorister, perhaps the legendary Thespis, stepped out to sing the words of the hero whose story formed the content of the song. As we see in Aeschylean drama, early tragedy, despite the availability then of two actors, was dominated by the chorus, with individual actors engaging in dialogue or debate

---

9 John Winkler, "The Ephebe's Song: *Tragoidia* and Polis," 20-62 in Winkler Zeitlin (1990). In support of Winkler see Wilson (2000) and Nagy (1995).

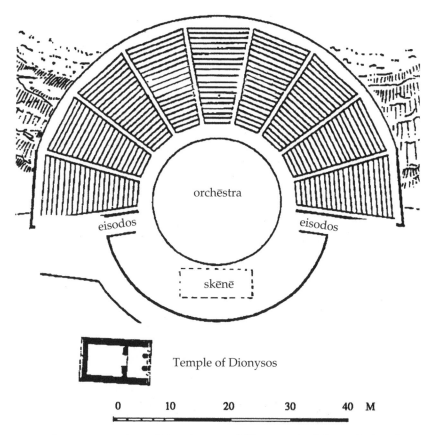

orchēstra

eisodos

eisodos

skēnē

Temple of Dionysos

| 0 | 10 | 20 | 30 | 40 | M |

A reconstruction of the theater of Dionysus in Athens during the second half of the fifth century BC. (Based on the sketch by J. Travlos, Pictorial Dictionary of Ancient Athens [London 1971] 540.)

with it; the only extended direct conversation between two actors in Aeschylus' *Agamemnon* is the great debate between Clytemnestra and her husband about whether he should walk on the scarlet cloths she has strewn in his path. The two earliest extant dramas by Euripides, the *Alcestis* (438 B.C.E.) and the *Medea* (431) both can work with only two actors, even though Sophocles had introduced the third actor roughly two decades earlier; even Aeschylus' *Agamemnon* (458) requires three actors. The *Medea* is the last extant tragic drama that can be performed with only two, and the final drama we have from the fifth century, Sophocles' *Oedipus at Colonus*, requires some extremely fancy foot-work, not to mention lightning-fast costume changes, to be performed with only three actors. But whether two or three were available, actors still had to be capable of embodying multiple parts in each production, across four different works in a single day, an achievement of as much physical endurance as artistic prowess; indeed, the sheer physical demands on the principal actors must have severely limited the available pool. They managed multiple roles, of course, through the use of costumes and simple, though realistic, masks, which likely represented types of characters who could be readily identifiable to audiences (e.g. the Old Pedagogue, the Adolescent Hero, the Virtuous Wife and Mother, the Nurse), many of whom only saw the masks at a great distance. Audiences could quickly identify the characters through a combination of these types and the habit of dramatists to signal immediately their identity through words ("I am Polydorus." "Look, here comes Odysseus.") The actors would also have already appeared, unmasked, alongside the poets at a ceremony called the *Proagon* (literally, the "before the contest") on the day before the three days of tragic performances.

While standing with his actors there in the Odeon of Pericles, next to the Theater of Dionysus itself, the dramatist would also announce the subjects of his dramas, which seem to have been invariably drawn from the traditional, heroic world of Greek myth. While we lack evidence that Athens consciously limited plot materials to myth, we do know that an early tragedian, Phrynichus, so upset the Athenians with a drama, *The Capture of Miletus,* depicting the destruction in 494 of a close ally at the hands of the Persians, that he was required to pay a large fine (Herodotus 6.21). Aeschylus managed to get away with a historical tragedy in *The Persians* because, first, he depicted the seminal victorious moment in Athenian history, their defeat of King Xerxes and his armies at Salamis, but also because he drew those events into recognizably mythic patterns and types. Every other tragic drama that we know relies on myth, but not on myth as a rigid, unchanging set of prescriptions, for the tragedians had enormous freedom to adapt myth to their needs. Aspects of myth that modern audiences tend to regard as canonical, such as the self-blinding of the Sophoclean Oedipus or the infanticidal Medea of Euripides, likely were innovations (and shocking ones at that!) by their authors. So long as the basic idea of the myth held, and Oedipus still kills his father and marries his mother, and the children of Medea die after Jason leaves his family, then the dramatists had a fairly free hand. They could even invent secondary characters, such as Polymestor in the *Hecuba,* and sometimes even major ones, as Sophocles seems to have done with Antigone. But the use of stories drawn from the legendary past does not necessarily mean that Athenian tragic drama was an escapist turn away from the problems of its present, and to the relation of tragedy to Athens we now turn.

DRAMA AND THE CITY OF ATHENS

While the City Dionysia and the institution of tragic drama was likely conceived, if not launched, under the reign of the tyrant Peisistratus during the sixth century B.C.E., the growth and final form of the dramatic festival seems to have been inextricably linked with the development of democratic *polis* of Athens in 508 B. C. E., for the City Dionysia became a quintessential instrument and expression of the democratic Athenian *polis*.[10] The first great Athenian dramatist, Aeschylus, fought at both Marathon and Salamis, the two great victories over Persia that launched the "golden age" of Athens, and he commemorated the latter defeat of foreign imperial tyranny in his *Persians*, in which the young Pericles served as the *choregos*, the wealthy citizen who underwrote the cost of training and outfitting the chorus for a whole year. Sophocles served the Athenian government in several capacities and staged the tensions of Athenian *polis* life through a number of his tragedies. Euripides played no known role in formal public life, and had the reputation of being something of a recluse, yet his dramas are full of the spirit and language of the Athenian Assembly and law courts, the other two great institutions of Athenian democracy.

The City Dionysia was a fundamentally civic institution, radically unlike anything in modern America. The festival as a whole was operated and funded by the state with the clear supervision of one of the nine *archontes*, the principal administrative officials of Athens; immediately following the festival's close there would be a public discussion in the Theater itself of its management at which the appropriate officials would be held accountable for any problems. The Dionysia, however, also provided rich citizens one of their few opportunities to display their wealth publicly in a required "contribution" (*leitourgia*) that gave them the choice of underwriting either the entire expense of the chorus for a playwright or a warship and its crew; this option shows the centrality of drama to Athens and the enormous cost of these single productions (and one might productively compare the cost of

---

10 On tragic drama and Athenian democracy see Goldhill (2000), Seaford (1994), and Connor (1989) and (1996). The cautions by Rhodes (2003) against the overemphasis on democracy, as opposed to the ideology of the *polis*, in studies of Athenian drama, are salutary.

a modern aircraft carrier with the budget for the American National Endowment for the Arts!). The festival thus enabled participation by the wealthy and display of their wealth, while also recognizing those who had served Athens well in the previous year and would serve it in the future. During the City Dionysia, the glory of Athens and its citizens was on full display. Before the tragedies, the ten generals of the Athenian army poured out libations to the gods in view of the audience, as part of a series of pre-performance spectacles. Member states of the Delian League, an alliance of city-states formed to punish Persia and guard against its renewed aggression but which quickly became a *de facto* empire for Athens, would annually pay financial "tribute" to Athens to fund the expenses of the alliance. Before the performance of the tragedies, in the Theater of Dionysus, Athenian officials would bring out the "talents" of silver (one talent=57 lbs. of silver coins) for the full crowd to see, a display of wealth and power that doubtless pleased many citizens in the audience but rankled visitors. At the same time, Athens paraded the sons of soldiers who had lost their lives in war and who had been raised at public expense. Athens then awarded, in the Theater, these youths with their own armor. Moreover, this same audience would witness the recognition of service to Athens with the award of golden crowns. The glory of Athens and its ideology were thus foregrounded and proclaimed in an event whose primary function was to produce theater.

In such a context, one would expect the dramas themselves to express unequivocally the value system or ideology of the Athenian *polis*, and yet nothing could be further from what one finds in the texts of the dramas, that, among other things, problematize, if not undermine, the subordination of familial concerns to the needs of the state; present admirable heroes whose competitive egoism clashes with the cooperative spirit of the democracy; and, especially during the last quarter of the fifth century when Athens engaged in its long conflict with Sparta, seem to question the reasons for and the conduct of war. Tragic drama was part of the public debate about the nature of Athenian society and government. Myth enabled playwrights to address social problems obliquely and in multifaceted ways. The form of drama, where issues are debated and no single voice has authority over the others, mirrors the very structure of the two foundations of Athenian democracy: freedom of speech (*parrhesia*) and equality (*isonomia*). The agents in these dramas often embody values that are contrary to these two ideals, and yet their language is steeped in the concepts and terminology of the audience. Were many Greek tragedies one-sided polemics on particular events of the day, such as, say, many of the films of Oliver Stone, they would not still be living works of art today, with the power both to move and to provoke.[11] Time and again, the Theater of Dionysus bears witness to debates over the fundamental questions of Athenian society (indeed, perhaps of any society) — the nature of justice, the place of women, the rights of suppliants, the nature of human freedom, the reasons for war — that seem equally or more appropriate for the Athenian Assembly and the law courts, and that suggest linkages between the three as forums for public speech. All three venues engaged in the mediating of conflicting social values through language. The Theater of Dionysus and the Pnyx (where the Assembly met) were the two settings for large-scale meetings of the Athenian people, and their physical natures were quite similar: semi-circular amphitheaters, at the bottom of which speakers would try to convince their auditors of the rightness of their case.[12] Some scenes in tragedy, such as the final one in Euripides' *Hecuba*, are self-consciously styled as legal trials, with set speeches for both prosecution and defense before a judge. Other tragic debates seem at first more personal and private, but only until one remembers the mass scale of the original audience and the requirements of acting in masks. Let us take two Sophoclean debates for examples, the confrontation between Oedipus and Creon early in the *Oedipus Tyrannus* and the argument over Ajax's burial between Teucer and Menelaus in the *Ajax*. If one were to hand the scripts to two modern actors working in a contemporary theater, they would stand nose-to-nose, yelling directly at each other, confident they could be heard by the 350 people in the darkened, indoor theater. Such an approach would not work with masks in an outdoor theater of 16,000 spectators. For the mask to engage its character and the character the audience, it must face forward. For the actor to be heard in a large outdoor space he must face the audience. Any significant turn to the side undermines the engagement of the mask and makes the actor substantially less audible. The actors must face forward and

11 As I completed work on this volume, the Royal Shakespeare Company produced Euripides' *Hecuba* in a new translation by Tony Harrison and starring the great actress Vanessa Redgrave. Both production and translation were criticized for their heavy-handed allusions to the invasion of Iraq by the United States in 2003. Such critics implied the work could speak to such concerns by itself, without the overemphasis on our contemporary world.

12 On the resemblance of the Pnyx and the Theater of Dionysus, see Josiah Ober and Barry Strauss' "Drama, Political Rhetoric and the Discourse of Athenian Democracy, " 237-270 in Winkler and Zeitlin (1990).

address the audience, and this position changes the debates from personal confrontations between two people to a set of speeches before an assembly or jury that argue the merits of the characters' positions. The actors address each other through the audience. The argument between Menelaus and Teucer is thus a public debate over the treatment of the bodies of warriors, and, during the trial scene of Euripides' *Hecuba*, Polymestor and Hecuba justify their actions not just to Agamemnon but to the audience as well, which thus becomes, in effect, a jury. The audience was part of the theatrical process. Drama was an integral part of the *polis* life of Athens.

ATHENIAN DRAMA AND THE PELOPONNESIAN WAR

Of the surviving tragedies of Euripides, only the *Alcestis* (438 B. C. E.) was produced outside of the shadow of the Peloponnesian War, which stretched from 431 to 404, ending with the defeat of Athens at the hands of its bitter enemy Sparta. The great danger for the modern reader here is in oversimplifying the relationship of ancient Greek drama to this conflict; one could leap to the conclusion on the basis of the depiction of suffering in Euripides' *Trojan Women* that Euripides must have been vehemently opposed to the war, or, one could look at the extended denunciations of Sparta in the earlier *Andromache* and leap in the opposite direction, ripping the speech out of its immediate context. Ancient Athenian playwrights, unlike, for example, modern film directors, are unknown to have ever held press conferences in which they hold court on their political views and the relationship of those views to their art. As discussed previously in this Introduction, ancient dramatists generally eschewed overtly political dramas with a contemporary basis for their plots. And yet, the sheer frequency of the themes of war, its causes and its effects in the Athenian Theater of Dionysus during the time of the Peloponnesian War indicates that the real war experienced by the members of the audience was energizing the presentation of myths of ancient wars by the actors in front of them. It is thus impossible to figure out definitively Sophocles' political position on the basis of the *Philoctetes*, produced late in the war (409 B. C. E.), but it is also, I think, impossible to overlook the similarity of the desperation of the Greek leaders (and of Philoctetes himself) late in the Trojan War with the growing desperation of Athens in its conflict with Sparta. In general, we can see Athenian drama, especially in Euripides' hands, reflecting the increasing levels of savagery throughout the Greek world during the war, as well as participating in the debate over certain issues raised by the war, through the prism of myth.

Euripides' *Trojan Women* (415), produced roughly a decade after the *Hecuba*, has been the traditional touchstone for scholarly considerations about Euripides and the Peloponnesian War. With its depiction of the suffering female victims who survive the destruction of Troy, the virtuoso display of sophistic rhetoric of Helen, who defends her conduct and the war itself as actually beneficial to Greece, and the climactic announcement of the brutal death of Hector's son Astyanax, this tragic drama clearly evokes, if not responds to the events of the Peloponnesian War. But which events? Scholars have suggested the events at Melos the year before or the looming invasion of Sicily. In 416 Athens "invited" the independent, neutral island of Melos to join its empire. Thucydides (5.84-113) presents a version of a dialogue that likely took place between the representatives of Athens and Melos that marks the former as advocating a particularly bleak and amoral version of "power politics" that had increasingly characterized the world of the Peloponesian War.[13] Following the refusal of the Melians to capitulate, Athens immediately commenced a siege, and in the winter before the production of Euripides' *Trojan Women*, "the Melians surrendered unconditionally to the Athenians, who put to death all the men of military age whom they took, and sold the women and children as slaves" (Thucydides 5.116). At around the same time, the Athenian assembly voted, after over fifteen years of war with Sparta, to invade, without a compelling cause, the larger island of Sicily, located six hundred miles away, with the largest armada they had ever assembled (Thucydides 6). Like the expedition against Melos, the attack on Sicily was unprovoked, but this incursion ended in total ruin and Athens never really recovered from it. The prologue of Euripides' tragedy forecasts the destruction of the great Greek armada as it leaves Troy, and thus it also perhaps prophesies that of the great Athenian fleet soon to sail for Sicily. So was *The Trojan Women* a protest against Athenian policy on Melos, an anticipation of the effects of Sicily? Both? Neither? While we lack evidence about the personal political position of Euripides during these years, it is difficult, for me at least, to believe Euripides could have written such an emotionally shattering drama as *The Trojan Women* without some kind of urgent impetus such as a reaction to the sufferings of the Melians.

Such was the situation a decade after Euripides' *Hecuba*, yet already in the mid 420s chaos was growing in the Greek world and Athens was grappling with unforeseen consequences to its military

---

13 On the relationship between Euripidean tragedy and Thucydides' depiction of the Peloponnesian War see the discussions of Hogan (1972) and J. Finley (1938).

policy, both of which seem reflected in the contemporaneous *Hecuba*. Among the atrocities committed by both sides during those years, Thucydides seems to have found the civil war (*stasis*) in Corcyra most disturbing and most exemplary. Corcyra, an Athenian ally, had fallen into internal upheaval that was exacerbated by interventions by both Sparta and Athens. Oligarchs and democrats fought in the streets and from the rooftops. Corcyra gradually slipped into anarchy. As Thucydides reports (3.81-2):[14]

> There was death in every shape and form. And, as usually happens in such situations, people went to every extreme and beyond it. There were fathers who killed their sons; men were dragged from the temples or butchered on the very altars; some were actually walled up in the temple of Dionysus and died there. So savage was the progress of this revolution, and it seemed all the more so because it was one of the first which had broken out. Later, of course, practically the whole of the Hellenic world was convulsed . . . [W]ar is a stern teacher; in depriving them of the power of easily satisfying their daily wants, it brings most people's minds down to the level of their actual circumstances. . . To fit in with the change of events, words, too, had to change their usual meanings. What used to be thought of as a thoughtless act of aggression was now regarded as the courage one would expect to find in a party member; to think of the future and wait was merely another way of saying one was a coward; any idea of moderation was just an attempt to disguise one's unmanly character; ability to understand a question from all sides meant that one was totally unfitted for action.

Thucydides continues along these lines for some time, but the reader of the *Hecuba* should find them already familiar, because Thucydides is describing the moral universe of Euripidean drama during these years. The phrase, "war is a stern teacher," is rendered more literally in two possible ways from the original Greek. The Greek words about the pedagogic effectiveness of war, *biaios didaskalos*, can mean "violent teacher" and "teacher of violence." The concern here, and elsewhere, in Thucydides with the relationship human nature and circumstances, is articulated also throughout Euripides' *Hecuba*. Hecuba herself, after hearing the depiction of the courage of her daughter Polyxena in the face of death, speculates how the growth of children in the face of

14 Translation by Rex Warner (Penguin. New York. 1954).

adversity is like and unlike the development of plants; how can her Polyxena be so noble in death when she has suffered so much? But Hecuba herself has had a *biaios didaskalos* and reacts to her children's deaths in way evocative of what Thucydides describes of the citizens of Corcyra, where women took part in the violence by hurling roof tiles down on members of the opposition (Thucydides 3.74). Moreover, Thucydides' account of the abuse of language, the self-serving shifts in rhetoric, resonates in Odysseus' justifications of human sacrifice and Polymestor's account of his "pre-emptive" murder of Polydorus.

The most exact and direct correlation between an episode in the Peloponnesian War and Euripides' *Hecuba* can be found in the events surrounding the city of Mytilene in 428-27, just before the Corcyrean civil war, and which occupies the first fifty chapters of Book 3 of Thucydides' *History*. The city of Mytilene on the island of Lesbos had allied itself with Sparta and had begun to force the rest of the island under their control, thus endangering the role of Athens there. But the revolt failed and thus Athens suddenly found itself, as does the Greek army in the scenario of Euripides' *Hecuba*, with a substantial number of prisoners of war, from which the furious Athenian Assembly voted to kill the entire male population and enslave the women and children (3.36). And yet, overnight, enough Assembly members had second thoughts about the rashness of their decision to kill the innocent along with the guilty, and there was thus a second debate about the prisoners, recorded by Thucydides, which featured the demagogue Cleon, one of Aristophanes' favorite targets, whom Thucydides notes was "remarkable among the Athenians for the violence of his character, and at this time he exercised far the greatest influence among the people." The twisted logic of Cleon's rhetoric, full of such hyperbolic claims as "no single city has ever done you the harm that Mytiline has done" (3.39), resonates in the Euripidean speeches of Odysseus and Polymestor. However, the more measured, merciful speech of Diodotus carried, barely, enough force so that only those guilty of the revolt were executed. A second boat was sent, which overtook its predecessor because the latter was rowing slowly due to the unpleasant nature of its mission.

As Justina Gregory has observed,[15] Euripides' *Hecuba* strongly echoes such debates, for the language of the drama's early scenes is steeped in the discourse of the Athenian Assembly, and the specious appeals to necessity in Odysseus' speech seem almost modeled directly on the similar claims Cleon makes in the debate over Mytiline.

---

15 Gregory (1999, 2002).

Euripides anachronistically has the Achaean army vote on human sacrifice in response to the reported demands of the ghost of Achilles. Hecuba's appeal for a reconsideration of the verdict (287-90) is based more on the parliamentary maneuver over Mytiline than anything in Greek myth. In those same lines, Hecuba herself questions the appropriate treatment of war prisoners, precisely the problem raised by the Mytilenian revolt. More importantly, such words raise the larger issue of the abuse of power by the victorious, an issue that continued for the Athenians well past the end of the war, into the attempts to deal with the treatment of Athenian aristocrats who had played roles in the coup of 411 and the oligarchic government that followed the defeat of Athens by Sparta in 404. Few lines in Greek tragedy are as salient to the decades of their immediate production and to our time as Hecuba's warnings to Odysseus on the need for the powerful to treat the conquered well because fortune will at some point turn (282-3), a maxim the drama itself supports with the later prophecies of Agamemnon's death, and the winds whipping up at the drama's close that both release the Greek ships and send them to their doom as the winds ripen into a maritime storm. Power must be related to justice. As Leonard Bernstein once said of the fruitlessness of Beethoven's hopes for universal brotherhood as expressed in his Ninth Symphony, "When, Lord, oh when?"

EURIPIDES' HECUBA

Euripides made his debut at the tragic competitions, one year after the death of Aeschylus, in the Athenian City Dionysia of 455 B.C.E., with a career that lasted roughly a half-century until his death, possibly in Macedon, in 406.[16] During the fifth century the Athenian drama "industry" produced over nine hundred tragedies, and the scholars of Alexandria in the third to second centuries B.C.E. attributed 92 of these to Euripides. Four of these were regarded then as spurious and of the remainder 78 survived intact to Alexandria to be gathered as the Collected Works. Eighteen plays (nineteen if we reject scholarly consensus that the *Rhesus* belongs to a now anonymous fourth-century playwright) have outlasted the dangers of existence on papyrus, parchment and paper. In antiquity scribes preserved poetry on rolls of papyrus which each could contain a single drama, collected alphabetically. It thus received priority during the Byzantine era, when it became, along with the *Phoenissae* and the *Orestes*, part of

---

16 See Scullion (2003) on the new doubts about this part of the biography of Euripides.

the "Byzantine Triad", the three most popular dramas of Euripides which were read by students at school. Such rankings were extended in time when manuscripts, preserved through the Middle Ages, began to be read during the Renaissance, which had already acquired a taste for bloody tragedies such as the *Hecuba* due to the influence of Senecan drama.

The *Hecuba* was composed by Euripides during the middle of his career, with the likely time of first production the mid to late 420s.[17] For the non-specialist reader, the difference between a production date of 425 and 423 is fairly insignificant, since the drama's psychological and moral world is not shaped by the events of any particular year, but by the more general crisis in the Athenian *polis* brought on by the Peloponnesian War (431-404) and by cultural forces such as the Sophists who had unleashed the power of rhetoric and questioned traditional conceptions of morality and religion. With its depiction of violent revenge by a female against her male oppressors, the *Hecuba* stands firmly in the model of Euripides' *Medea* roughly six to eight years before, and its characters and themes point forward to Euripides' (currently) more famous *Trojan Women* a decade later. It shares with both those dramas a concern with the power of persuasion. Its focus on the status of women, those out of power and at the margins of society, and it innovative use of myth characterize Euripides from his earliest extant drama, the *Alcestis* of 438, to his final tragedies, the *Bacchae* and the *Iphigenia at Aulis*, produced posthumously in 405.

THE CHARACTERS AND MYTH

Readers of this Greek tragedy, and of others, should always keep in mind that dramatists had a fair amount of freedom in their handling of myth; for example, Iphigenia might be hoisted on a sacrificial altar by her father, as Aeschylus's *Agamemnon* depicts, but she does not necessarily die, as seen in Euripides' *Iphigenia among the Taurians*, wherein she serves as a priestess to Artemis after the goddess had substituted a deer for her at the moment of death. Euripides is generally thought to have treated myth with much more freedom and self-consciousness than Aeschylus or Sophocles had.

In Euripides' *Hecuba*, three named characters should be familiar to a reader with a passing knowledge of Greek mythology and literature: Hecuba, Odysseus and Agamemnon. The concern here should

---

17 We cannot be sure of the exact year of the first production. The drama's metrical usage and content suggest a later date of roughly 423; see Collard (1991) 34-35, though Mossman (1992) 10-11 argues for an earlier date.

thus be with how Euripides' presentation of them resembles and differs from other texts. Three other characters, Polydorus, Polyxena and Talthybius, are mentioned elsewhere, but are typically not prominent, which leaves Polymestor, who is a creation, it appears, of Euripides. Let us briefly examine the characters in order of their appearance.

Polydorus. In the *Hecuba*, Polydorus is the last surviving son of Hecuba and Priam, while Homer makes him Priam's son by Laothoe and has him killed by Achilles near the start of his rampage following the death of Patroclus (*Iliad* 20.407). In both texts he is a young man, not a boy. Despite the differences in maternity and death, Euripides does remain true to the character's Homeric role in Priam's reported refusal to allow Polydorus to fight, and this tradition likely motivates Euripides' shift of Polydorus to safe-keeping in Thrace. Ghosts seldom appear in the surviving Greek tragedies, and thus likely made a great impact in the theater; Darius, an earlier king of Persia, features in *The Persians* (681) of Aeschylus, who also staged the appearance of the ghost of Clytemnestra (94) in *The Eumenides*. Apparently, Sophocles, in his lost *Polyxena*, brought on the ghost of Achilles as a speaking character.

Hecuba. The old widow of Priam, king of Troy, now a slave to Agamemnon, features most prominently in Books 6, 22 and 24 of Homer's *Iliad*. Her fierce maternal loyalties and protectiveness of her sons characterize her in Homer as in Euripides, though Euripides changes her lineage to make her the daughter of Cisseus, not Dymas (*Iliad* 6.299), with a Thracian lineage. Most poignant in Book 22 of the *Iliad* is her exposure of her maternal breasts, while utterly distraught at Hector's impending death, in the effort to convince Hector to come inside the Trojan walls to escape Achilles. Euripides does not veer far from Homer's depiction of Hecuba's ferocious hatred of her great son's destroyer (*Iliad* 24.212-14): "I wish I could bite into the middle of his liver and consume it." In both texts she is a suffering old woman, but not a completely passive figure, since she would defend her children at any cost to others and to herself. Polymestor's prophecy of her transformation into a dog is likely a Euripidean innovation; see the discussion in the notes below. In the *Hecuba*, she serves as Agamemnon's slave, while in *The Trojan Women*, produced roughly a decade later, she is assigned, much to her horror, to Odysseus.

Polyxena. The last virgin daughter of Hecuba and Priam; her sole surviving sister, Cassandra, has become Agamemnon's concubine. The tradition of her sacrifice by Neoptolemus at his father Achilles' tomb goes back at least as far as the lost epic *The Sack of Troy*, and another lost epic, *The Returns Home*, showed Achilles' ghost stopping the Greek fleet from departure. A poem by the lyric poet Simonides and a lost tragedy by Sophocles, *Polyxena*, also depicted Achilles' ghost demanding the sacrifice of Polyxena, a specific demand which is especially significant because the Euripidean drama does not name his desired victim. The shape of the larger Troy myth clearly creates a doublet for the sacrifice of Iphigenia in *Polyxena*; the repetition of virgin sacrifice provides closure to the Trojan War. Euripides returned to this subject at the end of his life in the *Iphigenia at Aulis*, with an Iphigenia who suddenly chooses death in sacrifice; indeed, Polyxena's speech at her sacrifice seems almost a dry run for Iphigenia's testimony (albeit more ironic) roughly twenty years later.

Odysseus. Achilles and Odysseus were the two greatest Greek warriors who fought at Troy. In the Homeric tradition he is renowned for his intelligence and his skill as an orator, though the *Odyssey* depicts him often as a trickster. While other sections of the larger Epic Cycle likely darkened the essentially ethical hero in Homer, his reliance on strategems and his persuasiveness made him, on the Athenian stage, a ready representative of the ideas of the Sophists or their students, the demagogic politicians of post-Periclean Athens. Odysseus' reported manipulation of the debate over the sacrifice of Polyxena, and his self-serving justification of the act to Hecuba, would have seemed all too familiar to the original Athenian audience.

Chorus of captive Trojan women. One of the striking paradoxes of Greek tragedy is that the communal voice of the Greek chorus often comes from characters who are not central members of the theater's community. While the male elders of the *Antigone* or *Oedipus Tyrannus* seem natural vehicles for communal sentiments to the all or overwhelmingly male audience, it might come as a surprise, given the context of performance, that the chorus is made up of slave women, prisoners of war before an audience whose members are grappling with what to do with prisoners in their own war.

Talthybius. Talthybius is known in the *Iliad* as the herald of Agamemnon whose "voice was like a god" (19.250). In this drama he delivers the first "messenger speech," a substantial narrative that occurs in almost every extant Greek drama, that allows the playwright to represent significant actions without a substantial change of scenery or to represent deaths that were not (or could not be) shown in the theater itself. This messenger speech is unusual in that it occurs very early in the dialogue (Polymestor's account of his punishment is another surrogate messenger speech) and in that its speaker is not anonymous. Since he, a common soldier, is the only Greek who displays both genuine pity for Hecuba and admiration for Polyxena, we might surmise that he is serving as a foil to show further the moral inadequacies of the Greek leaders.

Agamemnon. King of Argos and leader of the Greek army at Troy, Agamemnon here, as in virtually every other work of Greek literature in which he appears, is shown to be a weak, vacillating leader whose capabilities and character clearly are not suited to the demands of his responsibilities. Just as his selfish mistakes in Book 1 of Homer's *Iliad* unleash the wrath of Achilles, so too in Euripides' *Hecuba* he seems more determined to preserve his own position and keep his hands clean than to do the right thing.

Polymestor, king of Thracian Chersonese. There is no surviving evidence from antiquity of a Polymestor before Euripides' *Hecuba,* and Euripides does not given any ancestry to Polymestor, which further suggests Polymestor was his invention and characteristic of the plot's "Thracianized" content; Achilles' tomb is located in Homer (*Odyssey* 24.82) on the coast of Troy, across the Hellespont from where Euripides places it, and Euripides innovates Hecuba's ancestry to make it Thracian (perhaps to foreshadow her violent reaction to her son's murder). Euripides makes the setting of this drama integral with its events. Polymestor seems as harsh morally as the climate of the land that he rules, a climate that affects the Greek army when it votes for human sacrifice.

Plot and Unity

A summary: the ghost of Polydorus, son of King Priam and Queen Hecuba of Troy, forecasts the discovery of his corpse and the sacrifice of his sister Polyxena, serving alongside her mother as slaves, at the tomb of Achilles. When news reaches them of the decision to sacrifice Polyxena, Hecuba and her daughter lament her imminent death. Odysseus resists Hecuba's pleas to spare Polyxena or kill Hecuba herself instead. Polyxena surprises all by welcoming death as a liberation from slavery. The Greek herald Talthybius narrates the scene of Polyxena's death, where she shows great nobility and courage. Hecuba's grief is partially ameliorated by this report, and she prepares to see to Polyxena's burial, but when a corpse is brought in she discovers it is not her daughter but her last son, Polydorus, whom Priam had lodged with Polymestor, a king in Thrace, during the Trojan War. Polymestor, upon learning of Troy's fall, immediately murdered his guest in order to get his hands on the gold that had accompanied him for safekeeping. With the tacit complicity of Agamemnon, Hecuba plots her revenge against Polymestor by drawing him into her tent with the promise of news of more gold. Once inside, she and her fellow slaves murder Polymestor's children and blind him. The final scene is a trial in which Agamemnon rules in favor of Hecuba, but the drama dissolves into a furiously bitter exchange of denunciations until Polymestor prophesies both Hecuba's metamorphosis into a dog and Clytemnestra's murder of Agamemnon.

The plot thus falls into two parts and concerns have thus been raised about its unity. As Collard notes (21), "the plot is a revenge action developed from apparent helplessness," a type Euripides uses in *The Children of Heracles* and the *Orestes*. Yet other tragedies, such as the *Heracles*, show a similar essentially bifold division. Conditioned by the simpler, unified teleology of *Oedipus Tyrannus*, scholars have, until fairly recently, condemned such structures. Hecuba's seemingly sudden shift from helpless embodiment of despair to a figure of violent vengeance has contributed to these concerns; is the change in her credible, does she thus become as morally bankrupt as Polymestor, or is there even really a change?

Concerns about unity can be allayed by a greater attention to detail which reveals that the characters themselves see the deaths of Polyxena and Polydorus as linked, that Hecuba's words in the first half do not show a figure devoid of a desire to respond to suffering, and that the drama as a whole is a study in whether morality is conditioned by circumstances. Euripidean dramas typically open with a character who otherwise does not appear in the drama's action giving the background to the plot and an indication of what will occur over the next roughly 75-90 minutes, and the *Hecuba* is no exception, for Polydorus, after initially explaining his murder and the demands of Achilles' ghost, explicitly tells the audience that Hecuba will on this day see both Polyxena's corpse and his own. Euripides, however, does not indicate how, if at all, Hecuba will respond to this discovery. Agamemnon closes the drama with instructions to Hecuba to see to the burial of her children, thus bringing to fruition that early prophecy of Polydorus. The return of Polydorus as a dead body, visible to the audience for much of the second half, provides further signs of dramatic unity, as does the living body of Hecuba, out of sight only for two brief moments during the entire production; first (629-57) in reaction to the report of her daughter's death (and immediately before the arrival of Polydorus' corpse) and the second (1023-43) in order to prepare and perform her punishment of Polymestor. Moreover, Hecuba herself, as she begins to supplicate Agamemnon after the discovery of the murder, worries that (749-50), "Without this man I would not be able avenge my children." Hecuba clearly sees her subsequent actions as a single response to the two deaths.

The text also binds together the deaths of the children through parallel images and verbal echoes. Polydorus' position above the tent of his mother and his demands for a tomb foreshadows in the text's language (and recalls in the sequence of events) Achilles' appearance above his own tomb and demands for honor at that tomb (30-50). Hecuba's portentious dream of a wolf destroying a deer "slaughtered, rent from my knees without pity" (90-91) suggests both the death of Polyxena in its imagery of a victimized animal and the savage murder of Polydorus. The needs of the dead and the burial of children thus join the two actions together into a single movement.

Odysseus, both directly and indirectly, links the two halves of the drama. Directly, he plays a part in the sequence of two debate scenes that show Hecuba's progression from victim to avenger, from failed to successful persuader. A Greek audience would have recognized the structural parallels between the futile attempt to win Odysseus over to her side and her two-fold victory over Polymestor, first in persuading him to enter her tents and second in verbally conquering him in the trial scene at the end. These parallels become stronger, and richer in meaning, when we consider allusions to the *Odyssey* in the blinding of Polymestor and the very meaning of Polymestor's name. Let us consider his name first, by way of discussing two other related names. The prefix "poly-" is attached to the names of three characters here, Polyxena, Polydorus, and Polydorus, creating names that resonate in the themes and language of the drama as a whole. The Greek adjective *poludôros* in Homer means "bringing her family a great dowry,"[18] a meaning which, of course, would not apply to Polydorus but to his sister, and, in fact, Polyxena's future as a slave and not a bride who fetches a great price for her parents (350-66) figures prominently in her acceptance of her death, and, moreover, her death insures that she will only ever be the proverbial Bride of Hades, the girl who, like Persephone, marries Death. So his name is somewhat ironic, and this irony is furthered when we consider his name as also meaning

---

18 *Iliad* 6.394, *Odyssey* 24.294

"many gifts," and the text signals this meaning by the parallels between Polydorus, the man of many gifts who actually has none, and the Achilles who believes he is *adôrêtos*, "lacking gifts," when he is the most honored of all warriors. The name of his sister, Polyxena, functions similarly, as it means "the host of many." Walter Burkert has speculated that her name points to a possible ancient practice where, before a maiden was sacrificed, she had to offer herself to all participants in a hero's funeral.[19] While we cannot verify the relevance of this practice to the *Hecuba*, still her name points to the theme so important to this tragedy, the *xenia*, or guest-host relationship. While the *xenia* will be discussed fully below, for now it should be noted that an adjective cognate with Polyxena's name (*poluxenos*) is used elsewhere in Euripides as a description for the perfect host, Admetus (*Alcestis* 569), and her brother has been murdered by his own host. The names of Polydorus and Polyxena thus point to each other in a shared experience of the drama's themes.

The name Polymestor further unifies the action as it evokes Hecuba's opponent in her first debate, Odysseus, with her second, Polymestor himself. *Mêstôr* means counselor, adviser, or deviser; so *polumêstor* suggests "he who counsels much," or "the man with many devices." Both in sound and sense this strongly resembles *polumêtis* ("of many counsels or devices"), one of the epithets that most strongly characterizes Odysseus in Homeric epic.[20] As Justina Gregory has observed, one of the *Hecuba*'s primary concerns is with the separation of morality from power, and this schism figures most prominently in the actions of Polymestor and Odysseus; the latter manipulates the debate of the response to the vague demands of Achilles' ghost so that the sacrifice of Polyxena, who has already suffered greatly, suddenly becomes the only possible solution to their problems. Yet Euripides presents an Odysseus so utterly inhuman that he does not even argue that Polyxena must die in order for the fleet to depart; he simply argues for the need to honor an army's warriors as much as possible.[21] Odysseus' specious appeal to the need to preserve the viability of the warrior code is matched by Polymestor's justification of the murder by appeal to a future invasion of the region in order to

---

19 Burkert (1983) 67.
20 E.g. *Iliad* 1.311, 3.200, 4.329; *Odyssey* 2.173, 4.763, 5.214. Note, though, that *mêtis* and *mêstôr* derive from different verbs.
21 Mossman is succinct here, (1999) 117: "Euripides ruthlessly undercuts his moral standing by clever manipulation of the standard rhetorical ploys he gives him to speak." Mossman's book is valuable in many ways, not least for its examination of rhetoric.

find the last surviving son of Hecuba and Priam. Hecuba, however, is able to defeat the second man of many devices, because she has already shown his lust for gold and trapped him in an obvious show of duplicity.

A further link between Polymestor and Odysseus, though a more tangled one, is that Hecuba's blinding of Polymestor is modeled on Odysseus' of the Cyclops Polyphemus in Book 9 of Homer's *Odyssey*.[22] One needs to be careful about too exact a comparison here as otherwise one winds up with a pat formula like "Polyphemus=Polymestor, therefore Odysseus=Hecuba," which creates obvious problems in itself. It does, however, seem likely that Euripides wants us to see Hecuba adopting Odyssean guile here to mutilate a monstrous figure whose murderous behavior evokes the Cyclops, the eater of Odysseus' men and violator of the guest code. As Polymestor is made more inhuman as a result of the comparison, so is Hecuba elevated in stature. But I think the connection between the name of Polymestor and the epithet of Odysseus, combined with Hecuba's stated concern with avenging both of her children, shifts the impact of the allusion to the *Odyssey* to make her vengeance actual on Polymestor and symbolic on Odysseus. Moreover, the linkage of Polymestor and the Odyssean Polyphemus would be even more compelling and appropriate if, as some believe, Euripides' *Cyclops* was the satyr play that followed the *Hecuba* and the two other Euripidean tragedies that year.[23]

The trial scene, then, brings back the assembly and the world of Athens and re-inforces the larger arc of the action as a set of scenes mirrored in each half of the drama. Political debates and trial scenes, while anachronistic, are characteristic of Athenian drama. Athens had a fully developed court system and its language and concerns frequently appear in Athenian drama, starting with the trial of Orestes in the final part of Aeschylus' *Oresteia*, the *Eumenides*. Indeed, from the virgin sacrifice to female vengeance to the court scene itself, the *Hecuba* alludes to many aspects of the *Oresteia*.[24] Yet, just as the political assembly depicted in the first half of the *Hecuba* shows an ailing body politic easily manipulated by demagogues, so too does its end

---

22 See the essays on the *Hecuba* in Segal (1993) and Zeitlin (1996). Mossman's warnings (1999) 191-92 against oversimplifying the allusion are well heeded.

23 Thus argues William Arrowsmith in the introduction to his translation of the *Cyclops*, in *The Complete Greek Tragedies, Euripides*, volume 2, eds. D. Grene and R. Lattimore (Chicago 1956).

24 On the relationship between Euripides' *Hecuba* and Aeschylus's *Oresteia* see Thalmann (1993).

depict a trial that, unlike its Aeschylean prototype, does not prevent violence, but merely punishes it, and points to its continuation after the stage action has ended.

ABOUT THIS TRANSLATION

My goal here has been to produce a translation that has as little to do with me as possible; this means I do not introduce any new metaphors through the process of translation, I try to keep the English lines as close to their Greek counterparts in number and placement as I can without making the English excessively awkward, and I try to translate the Greek into English using the same English words consistently. This translation will thus not be the most poetic available (though I do sometimes strive to render Euripides' use of alliteration) and sometimes English idiom will be sacrificed to the goal of preserving the flow of ideas from the original Greek lines, though without, I hope, falling into the trap of "translationese." What is gained is a more accurate approximation of Euripides' Greek than has sometimes been the case in translations of the *Hecuba* so that readers can follow shifts in word use and language more coherently. Another result of a more literal translation is that English words will now show Euripides' insistence on certain key themes as embodied in the drama's language. For example, the Greek idiom *didômi dikên* is normally translated as "I pay the penalty (for transgression)", and rightly so, since it connotes punishment. But it literally means "I give justice." Justice (*dikê*) is, arguably, the most important theme in the play, and this idiom thus allows the audience to hear "justice" repeatedly. I believe that English readers need to see (and hear) this insistence preserved, so I have compromised with the translation "to pay justice." Similarly, Euripides uses two words to denote Hecuba's children, *teknon*, which I have translated as "child," and *pais*, which I have translated as "boy" for Polydorus and "daughter" for Polyxena; "boy" in English, coming from a mother, has a much greater emotional range, I think, than just "son." It connotes Polydorus' child-like helplessness against the machinations of his host, and a mother's despair over losing the one son, her "baby," she believed was safe.

One of the difficulties of translating Greek tragedy for a modern audience is that modern American English has an impoverished vocabulary for lamentation. "Alas" is, at best, extremely stilted, and, at worst, inducing of giggles. Thus, when I do chose to translate *pheu* as "alas", that is when I feel a character's stated grief is insincere. Other terms of grief, such as *aiai* or *oimoi*, I leave untranslated, since the inarticulate interjections seem, in some ways, more powerful than any actual English equivalent.

The first readers of this translation were the students in my introductory Greek Drama and Culture course in the spring of 2002 at Temple University. I inflicted an extremely awkward first draft on them, and asked them to help me write the notes and commentary by telling me what they needed to know. As complete novices, they were the best judges of what other students would need in the final edition. I am extremely grateful to them for their help.

These students also helped me with the stage directions, and about stage directions I must also say a few words. The manuscripts that led to modern editions lacked any stage directions, and, indeed, even changes in speaker were indicated by simple marks. Any stage direction in a modern translation comes from the translator's imaginative interaction with the contents of the play itself. Some directions, such as indications of a speaker's tone, are more imaginative than others. Readers who consult multiple translations will find wide differences in matters such as when exits occur and in what direction. Some of my stage directions will raise eyebrows, but I have tried to indicate which directions are more imaginative than others; in general, they are based on information in the text and from my working on possible dramatic reconstructions with my students. One last note about directions: directions are given according to the audience's perspective, and so, for example, "right" is the audience's right.

Readers will notice that some passages are placed inside brackets. These are used to represent where modern editors have reached a conclusion that a part of the received manuscript is not genuine; those lines were added subsequently, usually by actors. These additions are called interpolations.

I am here indebted to many people, both through their scholarship and through their direct assistance to me. My Greek text, unless otherwise noted, has been Justina Gregory's splendid edition from 1999. In preparing this translation and commentary I have learned not just from Professor Gregory's wisdom in her Greek edition, but also from the earlier commentary of Christopher Collard. I stand firmly and gratefully on their shoulders. Revisions to my first manuscript were made during a happy period as Visiting Fellow at Wolfson College, Cambridge and Visiting Scholar in the Faculty of Classics at the University of Cambridge; I am thus especially full of thanks to Robin Osborne and Pat Easterling for facilitating my Fellowship, and to Temple University for a Study Leave to fund my Cambridge sojourn. Last, I am grateful to Peter Meineck for helping me think about the important of performance in general a decade ago, and to Stephen Esposito for his initial encouragement and his comments on an earlier draft.

The Structure of Euripides' *Hecuba*

1-215   Prologue and lyric lament: the announcement of the deaths of Hecuba's children Polydorus (past) and Polyxena (future).

  1-58   Speech of the ghost of Polydorus

  59-97   Hecuba's monody (solo song) on her nightmare prophesying the death of Polydorus

  98-152   parodos (choral entry song) on the apparition of Achilles and the army's vote to sacrifice Polyxena

  154-215   lyric lament and dialogue of Hecuba and Polyxena

    154-76   Hecuba's reaction to news from Chorus

    177-96   Polyxena forces Hecuba to reveal this news

    197-215   Polyxena's distress over her mother's sorrow

216-443   First episode: the debate over the sacrifice of Polyxena (debate 1)

  216-33   Odysseus' speech on the army's debt to Achilles and Hecuba's response

  334-443   Polyxena's decision to accept death, and her farewell to her mother

444-83   First Choral Song: on the destiny of slaves

  444-54   *strophe a*: Chorus wonders where they will be taken and what will they do in their new homes (Doris, Phthia)

  455-65   *antistrophe a*: continuation of speculation (Delos)

25

953-1295 Fourth Episode and Exodus: Revenge against Polymestor
and Trial Scene (debate 2)

953-1022   Hecuba lures Polymestor and sons into her
tent, where she and the other women blind
him and murder his sons

1023-34   Brief act-dividing lyrics praising Hecuba and
denouncing Polymestor

1035-1295 Exodus

1035-55   Polymestor blinded

1056-1108   Polymestor's monody (solo song)

1109-1295   trial of both Polymestor and
Hecuba with Agamemnon as
judge. Prophecies of Polymestor
after he is sentenced.

Euripides: *Hecuba*

Scene: An encampment on the shore of Chersonese in Thrace, shortly after the fall of Troy. Dawn is about to break. The skênê *is a simple tent, which serves as the living quarters of the slaves of Agamemnon. The right entrance way leads to the soldiers' camps, the left to Thrace and the sea.*

Characters and Distribution of Parts Among Three Actors[1]

Ghost of Polydorus, the last surviving son of Hecuba and Priam (**tritagonist**)

Hecuba, the old widow of Priam, king of Troy, now a slave to Agamemnon (**protagonist**)

Captive Trojan women, mute actors

Chorus of captive Trojan women

Polyxena, the youngest daughter of Hecuba and Priam, still a virgin (**deuteragonist**)

Odysseus, the greatest surviving Greek warrior, renowned for his intelligence and speech (**tritagonist**)

Talthybius, a minor Greek warrior who serves as a herald for King Agamemnon (**tritagonist**)

Serving maid of Hecuba (**deuteragonist**)

---

1 We have no records for which of the three actors were assigned to which characters, so we construct the assignments by which characters do not appear at the same time. The most talented actor was the protagonist (literally, the "first" actor), the second, the deuteragonist, and the third the tritagonist. While thematic and structural parallels make assigning the deuteragonist to Odysseus and Polymestor very tempting, the lengthy songs sung by Polyxena and Polymestor suggest those two extremely different characters were performed by a deuteragonist who specialized in such emotional monodies; likely, though by no means certain.

Agamemnon, King of Argos and leader of Greek army at Troy
(**tritagonist**)

Attendants of Agamemnon, mute actors

Polymestor, King of Thracian Chersonese (**deuteragonist**)

Sons of Polymestor, mute actors

The ghost of Polydorus appears above the skênê.[2]

GHOST OF POLYDORUS
>I am here after leaving the hiding places of corpses and the
>   gates of shadow
>where Hades dwells apart from the gods,[3]
>I, Polydorus, was the child of Cisseus' daughter, Hecuba,
>and Priam was my father,[4] who, when there was danger that
>the Phrygians'[5] city fall by Greek spears,   5
>terrified, in secret he sent me from the Trojan land
>towards the house of Polymestor, our Trojan guest-friend,[6]

---

2 He makes reference to being "above" his mother at line 29, and his needs
for a tomb seem to parallel and comment upon the desire of Achilles
for honor to be given to his tomb, and Achilles is said to have appeared
above it. The area above the *skênê* is generally reserved for gods. Among
the surviving Greek dramas, the *Hecuba* uniquely begins with a speech
by a ghost. Sophocles' lost *Polyxena,* the likely model for this drama,
almost certainly commenced with a solo speech by the ghost of Achilles.
The ghost here suggests the work of mysterious powers otherwise
unvoiced throughout the *Hecuba,* establishes a certainty that highlights
the ignorance of the living characters, and symbolizes a problematic
past, remembered, and then effaced.

3 Technically one of the Olympian generation of gods, Hades, a name
which designates both the lord of the Underworld and the place itself,
is kept apart from his peers who inhabit the sky.

4 Priam, as King of Troy, was one of the most powerful and wealthy rulers
in Greek myth, who, in the *Iliad,* sees all of his sons save Paris cut down
by Achilles.

5 Phrygia was a large, fairly undefined geographical area that encompassed
much of west-central Anatolia in Asia Minor. In the *Hecuba* "Phrygian"
is used interchangeably with "Trojan."

6 *Xenos.* See Introduction and Interpretive Essay on the importance of
the guest-host relationship in Greek ethics. Euripides here immediately
stresses that Polymestor violates the fundamental morals of Greek
society.

who cultivates this most fertile Chersonian land which you
    see here,[7]
ruling his horse-loving people by the spear.
My father secretly sent much gold with me,   10
so that, if ever Ilium's[8] walls should fall,
then his living sons would not lack livelihood.
Since I was the youngest of Priam's sons, he also sent me
furtively from the land; for I was able to bear neither armor
nor a spear with my young arm.   15
So while the country's walls remained upright,
and the towers of the Trojan land were intact,
and Hector[9] my brother was fortunate with his spear,
I grew quite well with the Thracian man, my father's guest-
    friend,
with upbringing like some sapling — a wretch;   20
but when Troy and Hector's life are
lost,[10] and the hearth of my fathers was razed,
and Priam himself before the god-founded altar falls
slaughtered[11] by Achilles' son,[12] desecrated with blood,
my father's guest-friend then slays me,
long-suffering, for the sake of gold,   25
and, after the slaying, to the salty swell

---

7 The Chersonese is a peninsula of Thrace that runs along the Hellespont,
making it a natural stop-over for ships sailing from Troy towards the
Greek mainland.

8 Ilium is another name for Troy.

9 Hector was the greatest of the Trojan warriors. His death at the hands
of Achilles, after his parents Priam and Hecuba beg him to enter the city
walls for safety, is the climax of Homer's *Iliad*.

10 Greek usage frequently retains for vividness a present tense when
narrating a past action. I attempt to retain this practice here and in other
sections of this drama.

11 The verb denotes sacrificial killing. Seaford (1994) 340 observes, "murder
in tragedy is generally envisaged as sacrifice."

12 Neoptolemus was summoned by Odysseus from his home in Skyros
after the death of his father. At the fall of Troy, Neoptolemus murdered
Priam at an altar in his own house, in front of his family, an episode the
Roman poet Vergil later depicts at *Aeneid* 2.506-58. Neoptolemus thus
moves from literally sacrificing Polyxena to a gross perversion of the
sacrificial act when he murders her father.

he released me, so that he himself could keep the gold in his
    house.[13]
And I lie upon the shore, sometimes in the sea's tossing,
borne along by the many cycles of the waves,
unlamented, unburied. But now above my mother,   30
Hecuba, I float, having abandoned my body,
suspended now already for a third day,[14]
for as long as in this Chersonesian land
my ill-starred mother from Troy has been present.
And all the Achaean ships at rest   35
lie thick on the shores of the Thracian land here;
for the son of Peleus[15] appeared above his tomb
and Achilles checked the entire Greek army,
although they were directing their sea voyage homewards.
He demands to take my sister Polyxena   40
as a blood-victim for his own tomb and a prize.
And he will obtain this, and from his men friends[16]
he will not lack gifts; the assigned destiny drives
my sister to die on this day.
Two corpses of two children,   45
my mother will behold, my own and her ill-starred daughter,
because I will appear in the surf at the feet of a slave-woman,

---

13 Virgil presents a slightly different version of the murder of Polydorus
   (*Aeneid* 3.22-67) in which his corpse, covered in protruding wooden
   spears, is transformed into a bush, and when Aeneas arrives and tugs
   at a branch he finds blood oozing from the plant and the plaintive voice
   of Polydorus begging for burial.

14 Greek time-counting is inclusive, so Polydorus has been aloft for two
   days since his murder, with the time of the play being the dawning of the
   third day. Collard notes, "the number three implies ritual or mysterious
   significance." For example, in the *Iliad* Patroclus makes three attempts at
   the walls of Troy before Apollo intervenes, and Achilles chases Hector
   around Troy three times before their duel.

15 Achilles. Homer had located Achilles' tomb at Sigrum on the coast of
   Troy (*Odyssey* 24.82). On the conflicting accounts of the location of the
   tomb see Pantelis (2002) 68-69.

16 "Men friends" warrants explanation. *Andrôn philôn* is much more highly
   gendered than merely *philôn*, which would have sufficed in itself to
   designate the reciprocal bonds of heroic society. The addition of *andrôn*
   ("men," dictionary form is *anêr*) speaks to the codes of heroic masculinity
   that are brutally indifferent to the needs of Hecuba and Polyxena.

so that, wretch that I am, I can get a grave;
for I demanded the powers below that I
acquire a grave and fall to my mother's hands.   50
So this will be mine, as much as I wished it to happen.
But I'll now withdraw[17] away from aged
Hecuba, for she here passes from behind the tent of
Agamemnon, fearing my phantom.

(Hecuba enters from inside the tent through the skênê *door, supported by
two women, who serve as slaves alongside their former queen.)*

Oh —
Oh you, mother who, though born from ruling households,
saw slavery's day, how your current misery
matches your previous success; and some one of the gods
ruins you in repayment for your earlier prosperity.

HECUBA[18]

Lead the old woman from the house, children.
Lead your fellow slave lifting her up,   60
once your queen, you women of Troy.
[Take, bear, send, lift me]
grasping my aged hand.
And I, leaning on the twisted staff with my hand,   65
I will speed the slow-footed step
of my joints, placing it out in front of me.

Oh blinding light of Zeus, Oh shadowy night,[19]
why ever am I carried away at night thus
by fears, by phantoms? Oh mistress Earth,   70
mother of black-winged dreams,

---

17 Polydorus possibly exits through a trapdoor on the roof of the *skênê*; see
Mastronarde (1990) 259-60 for the ways he could leave that area.

18 Hecuba here sings a monody. Gregory (1999) notes this song resembles
"a pattern also found in the *Ion*, the opening monologue spoken
by a supernatural character is followed by a solo aria sung by the
protagonist." This solo replaces the more typical choral entry song, which
is thus transformed into a lyrical exchange with Hecuba concerning the
sacrifice of Polyxena.

19 A number of tragedies, most famously the *Agamemnon* and *Antigone*
begin their actions just as the day breaks. Such settings suggest that
these dramas, including the *Hecuba*, were performed first in their trilogic
group. Each day's performances at the City Dionysia began at dawn.

I send back the nocturnal vision,
[which, through dreams, I saw, learned and understood
as a fearful vision concerning my child kept safe at Thrace,   75
and about my dear daughter Polyxena.]

Oh gods of the earth, save my boy,
who, the sole remaining anchor of my house,
inhabits snowy Thrace   80
under protection of his father's guest-friend.

Something new will happen;
some mournful song will come to mourning women.
Not ever has my spirit so incessantly
shuddered, feared.   85
When ever could I see the god-like mind of Helenus
and Cassandra,[20] Trojan women,
so they might discern these dreams for me?

For I saw a dappled deer by the wolf's bloody claw   90
slaughtered, rent from my knees without pity.
And this is my fear now: Achilles' phantom
came above the high crest of the tomb.
He was demanding as a prize
some one of the many-troubled Trojan women.   95
So from my, from my girl,
send this thing away, you gods, I beg you.[21]

CHORUS *(entering from right; the rhythm of their words is a recitative)*[22]

Hecuba, quickly to you I drew away,

---

20 Helenus and Cassandra were children of Priam and Hecuba who were
    also prophets. Cassandra was made a prophet by Apollo in exchange for
    sexual favors. When she refused him, he spat in her mouth and made
    her prophecies unbelievable to all who heard them. Helenus is praised
    in the *Iliad* (6.77) as "the best of the seers."
21 Most editors reject lines 90-7 as inauthentic. I follow Gregory's arguments
    in retaining them.
22 By "recitative" I mean a type of song that is more chanted than sung,
    here in the anapestic meter which was originally for marching and
    often thus used to accompany arrivals and departures (although 59-67
    of Hecuba's preceding monody was also in anapests). In general, this
    is the choral song called a *parodos*, which the chorus sings "along the
    way" as it enters the orchestra.

leaving our master's tents,
where I have been alotted and assigned as   100
slave, driven away from the city
of Ilium, at the lance's point,
spear-hunted by the Achaeans,[23]
relieving nothing of your sufferings,
but bearing a heavy burden of   105
news to you, lady, a herald of pains.
For in the full assembly of the Achaeans
it is resolved[24] that your daughter will be a sacrifice to
Achilles; you know when he mounted his tomb,
and appeared with golden weapons,   110
and he checked the sea-faring flotilla
whose sails strained at their ropes,
shouting out this: Greeks,
"Where, then, Danaans, do you think you're going,
leaving my tomb without a prize?"[25]   115
A wave of great strife crashed down together,
rumor ran asunder through the Greeks'
army of spearmen; to some it seemed best to give
blood-sacrifice to the tomb, while to others it didn't.
But there was one looking after your welfare,   120
the one keeping the god-visited Bacchant's[26]
bed, Agamemnon.
And the two sons of Theseus, the budding shoots of Athens,

---

23 The term Achaeans designates the people we call Greek who fought at
   Troy. It is interchangeable here with Danaans below.
24 This is a legislative formula from the Athenian assembly, applied here
   anachronistically. On the role of contemporary political terms from the
   Assembly see Michelini (1987) 143-44 and Hogan (1972) 250-51. Gregory
   (1999) 58 and (2002) discusses how the language of the contemporary
   Athenian assembly draws connections between the mythical past of the
   story and the political present of the audience.
25 The Homeric Achilles had been obsessed with honor and its visible tan-
   gible signs, such as war booty. His desire for more, even from beyond
   the grave, marks him as avaricious, characterized by the same greed
   that characterizes Polymestor's lust for gold.
26 Cassandra is technically not a female follower of the god Dionysus, as
   the designation "Bacchant" suggests, yet the wildness of her prophetic
   ravings would have made her resemble one.

were orators of double speeches;[27]
but they agreed in one sentiment,   125
to garland Achilles' tomb
with fresh greenery of blood, but they said they'd never
prefer the bed of Cassandra
to the spear of Achilles.
The efforts of the contested speeches   130
were somehow equal, until the shifty-minded
sweet-talking, crowd-pleasing liar,
the son of Laertes,[28] persuades the army
not to reject the best of all the Danaans
because of a slave's sacrifice,   135
nor that anyone of the dead
standing by Persephone[29] should say
how from Troy's plains
Danaans departed ungrateful to Danaans
who came on behalf of Greeks.[30]   140
Odysseus will come quite soon
to drag your foal from your breasts
and launch her from your aged hand.
But go to temples, go to altars,
[sit suppliant at Agamemnon's knees,]   145
call on the gods in heaven and
those below the earth!
For either prayers will prevent you
from being bereft of your unhappy child,
or you must behold her cast down on the tomb,   150
a virgin blood-reddened

27 Acamas and Demophon, the sons of Theseus by Phaedra. The mention
    of Athens and its greatest hero further links the action to contemporary
    Athens; see Michelini (1987) 142-43.
28 Odysseus. Although the hero of one of the two great Homeric epics, in
    the fifth century Odysseus' persuasive abilities lent him easily to being
    characterized in a manner that would suggest a Sophist or a demagogic
    Athenian politician.
29 The Queen of the Underworld and wife of Hades.
30 The *Iliad* betrays no sense of such nationalism among the Achaean
    warriors, who see themselves more as a loose confederation under
    Agamemnon's authority.

by a black-gleaming stream
from her gold-bearing neck.
HECUBA (*singing in lyric meters*)   (*strophe*)³¹
How unhappy I am! what ever should I shout?
What kind of cry? what lament?   155
Wretched woman of wretched old age,
of slavery not endurable,
not bearable? *oimoi moi.*
Who protects me? What family?
What city? Gone is my old man,   160
gone my sons.
What path do I take, this way or that?
Where is there some one of the gods
or spirits to help me?
Oh, you've brought suffering   165
Trojan women, you've brought suffering and
pains, you have destroyed and destroyed me utterly;
no longer is my life
admirable in the light.
Oh wretched foot, lead,   170
lead me, aged, to this hall here; Oh child, Oh daughter
of a most grievous mother — come out, come out
of the house — hear your mother's voice.
[Oh child, come out so that you may know
what, what sort of report I hear   175
about your life.]

Polyxena enters from the skênê. *She must be carrying or wearing some kind
of special clothing, as she instructs Odysseus to help her with her robes just
before she departs. This exchange occurs in irregular lyrical dialogue.*

POLYXENA
Ah.
Mother, mother, why do you cry? Heralding
what news have you flushed me from the house
like a bird with this terror?

---

31 Lyrical passages in tragedy are typically structured through organized,
  balanced pairs of strophe and antistrophe. There is no antistrophe in
  Hecuba's song; rather, Polyxena's subsequent lament (197-215) provides
  the response, matching her mother's song in form.

HECUBA

Oh my child!   180

POLYXENA

Why do you mourn me? The prelude seems bad for me.

HECUBA

Aaiai your life!

POLYXENA

Out with it! Don't hide it any longer.

I fear, I fear, mother,

why ever do you raise your lament...   185

HECUBA

Oh child, child of an unhappy mother...

POLYXENA

But what is this thing you will announce?

HECUBA

Your slaughter — the collective wisdom of the Argives

assigns you to the tomb

for the son of Peleus.   190

POLYXENA

Oh no, mother! What do you mean?

Explain those sad troubles to me,

mother, explain them!³²

HECUBA

I proclaim, daughter, ill-spoken rumors;

they announce to me the judgment of the Argives'   195

vote about your life.

POLYXENA   *(antistrophe)*

Oh terribly suffering one, Oh all-enduring,

Oh mother of a wretched existence!

Such, such an outrage

despised and unspeakable   200

has some god sent you.

No longer here by you, no longer

a wretched child by a wretched old woman

shall I share slavery.

---

32 There are punctuation difficulties in the Greek here.

For you will see me like a mountain-bred calf,   205
you wretched will see me a wretched sapling
....................[33]

torn from your hand and
cut at the throat, sent down under earth
to the gloom in Hades, where with corpses
I wretchedly shall lie.[34]   210

[And miserable you, mother,   *I'd rathe die?*
I mourn you with tear-drenched dirges,
but for my life, its outrage and mutilation,   *✓*
my lament takes no part, but a stronger fortune has fallen
to me to die]   215

CHORUS

And now look: Odysseus comes hurriedly by foot,
Hecuba, to signal some new story to you.

ODYSSEUS (*entering from the right. Odysseus then stands between
Polyxena and Hecuba, almost as a judge who hears both sides of a debate*)

Lady! I think you know the army's decision
and that the vote is final; but still I shall speak.
It seemed best to the Achaeans to sacrifice   220
your daughter Polyxena at the high mound of Achilles' tomb.
They assign us to be the escort and collector of the maiden.
The administrator and priest of the sacrifice
will be the son of Achilles.
So you know what you must do. Don't be torn away by
  force   *don't lament me of?*   225
and don't come into some scuffle of hands with me;
Consider your defenses and the presence of your
troubles. It's a wise[35] thing to keep your wits even in troubles
  that compel.

---

33 There is a gap in the manuscript here.
34 Note how Polyxena here, remarkably, worries more about her mother's
   suffering than her own death, but this magnanimity prepares her noble
   behavior at the sacrifice.
35 The Greek word *sophos* can mean wise or clever. Many texts from this
   era, especially Euripides' *Medea*, play off this ambiguity.

HECUBA

Aiai. A great trial[36] is at hand here, it seems,
full of groans and not empty of tears.   230
And I, at least, did not die when it was necessary that I die,
nor did Zeus destroy me, but he sustains me, so that I see
other troubles greater than troubles — I the wretched one.
But if it is possible for slaves to raise questions to free men,
neither painful nor biting the heart,   235
then it's necessary for you to respond in turn
and for us who ask these things to listen .

ODYSSEUS

It is possible. Ask away. I don't begrudge you the time.

HECUBA

Do you remember, when you came as a spy to Troy,[37]
shapeless in rags, and from your eyes   240
drops of blood dripped down your chin?

ODYSSEUS

I remember; it didn't just touch the edge of my heart.

HECUBA

And Helen recognized you and informed me alone?

ODYSSEUS

We remember that we'd come into great peril.

HECUBA

And as a humble man you touched my knees?[38]   245

---

36 *megas agôn.* The *agôn*, a highly stylized rhetorical debate, is central to many
    Greek dramas, especially in Euripides. The debate here foreshadows the
    later one between Polymestor and Hecuba, and this mirroring would
    mark Hecuba's reversal from powerless victim to powerful avenger. On
    Euripides' use of the *agôn* see Lloyd (1992).

37 The story of Odysseus' reconnaissance mission to Troy is told in *Odyssey*
    4.235-64, though there it is Helen alone who recognizes him and Hecuba
    is not mentioned. Note that Odysseus' disguise as a blind man with
    bloody eyes foreshadows Hecuba's real punishment of Polymestor.

38 The touching of the knees is part of the gesture of supplication, a
    condition that should guarantee the safety of the supplicator. For
    supplication scenes in Greek literature, see Gould's classic article *Hiketeia*,
    which has been reprinted with an addendum in Gould (2001) 22-77.
    Gould observes (23) that supplication "is essentially an act which seeks
    a *reciprocal* act on the part of him to whom it is addressed, above and
    beyond the concepts of reciprocity which are built into the structure of
    Greek social relationships."

ODYSSEUS

So that my hand grew still as death on your robes.

HECUBA

What, indeed, did you say then as my slave?

ODYSSEUS

The inventions of many words, so that I not die.

HECUBA

And then I saved you and sent you out of the land?

ODYSSEUS

So that I see this light of the sun now.   250

HECUBA

Are you not therefore ashamed at these plans,
you who experienced such things at my hands as you claim you
    experienced,
but you treat us not well, yet as badly as you can?
Ungrateful is your race, you who value the
demagogue's honors; would that you were not known to me, 255
you who, when harming your friends, don't worry,
if you would say something currying favor to the mob.[39]
But yet why, believing this to be a clever thing,
did they set a vote of murder against my daughter?
Was it that necessity compelled them to human sacrifice   260
at a tomb, where it's more normal to kill cattle?
Or was it that the desire to pay back the killers of Achilles
with killing justly aims murder against her?
But this girl did nothing wrong to him.
[Helen is the one he ought to request as sacrifice for
    his grave.   265
That woman destroyed him and drove him to Troy.][40]
But if it's necessary that some one of the spear-won women die,
and one surpassing in beauty, this shouldn't come from us:

---

39 These words reflect the growing sense in Athens that the Assembly
    had, following the death of Pericles, become too much under the sway
    of skillful speakers who could manipulate the people for their own
    personal ends without any concern for the greater good.

40 I accept Gregory's arguments here, following Kovacs, against the
    authenticity of these two lines.

the daughter of Tyndareus[41] is most splendid in form,
and she was found to be committing wrong no less than us.   270
    I set this argument in the competition for justice;
listen now to the things which you must answer back
when I demand. You touched my hand, as you say,
and this grey cheek in supplication;

(Hecuba reaches out to Odysseus)

In return I lay hold of the same parts of you   275
and I demand back the favor from then and I beg you,
that you don't tear my child from my hands.
Don't kill her! Enough are dead!
In her I have joy and forget my troubles;
this girl is my consolation in place of many: 280
city, nurse, crutch, journey's leader.
There is no need for rulers to rule what they need not,
nor for the lucky to believe they will always succeed;
for I was once also, yet I no longer am,
but a single day removed all blessings from me.   285
Still, oh face of a friend, show some reverence[42] for me,
give pity. Go to the Achaean army
and dissuade them, since there's jealous anger[43] at killing
women whom you didn't kill earlier when
you tore them from their altars, but you pitied then.   290
Among you there is a custom of equality
to free men and slaves concerning blood.[44]

appeal to Odysseus

41 Helen, like many male heroes, had two fathers, the divine Zeus and the
mortal Tyndareus. Hecuba seems to want to deny Helen's divine lineage
here by stressing her mortal father.

42 The verb here is a cognate of the noun *aidôs*, a Greek word that English
cannot represent with any single term. It communicates a sense of
reciprocal sense of honor, shame, respect and what is owed. Context
typically determines which of those senses are predominant in a
particular usage. See Cairns (1993) and the discussion in the Interpretive
Essay of this volume. Of course, Odysseus is not a "friend," but the
adjective here, *philos*, connotes the reciprocal bonds that he should feel
from their previous relationship.

43 *Phthonos* is the jealous anger of the gods at excessive human success.

44 This is an anachronistic appeal to Greek law in general and fifth-century
Athenian law in particular; by using the terms *isos* (equal) and *nomos* (law)
together Hecuba unknowingly evokes for the audience their treasured
principle of *isonomia*, a bedrock of Athenian democracy which guaranteed
equal protection of the laws and equal participation in politics.

Your status, even if you should speak badly,
will persuade; for a speech coming from the disreputable
is not as strong as the same one coming from the reputable.   295

CHORUS
A man's nature is never so rigid
that, hearing your groans and lamentations
of long weepings, it would not shed a tear.

ODYSSEUS
Hecuba, accept my instruction and don't by your anger make
the one who speaks favorably hostile in his thoughts.   300
I am ready to save your bodily life, at whose hands I've been
fortunate, and I don't speak in vain.
And what I said to all I will not deny:
since Troy has been sacked we give your daughter
as a sacrifice to the first man of the army as he demands.   305
For in this matter many cities struggle,
whenever some man, though noble and eager,
still takes away nothing more than his inferiors.
But to us Achilles is worthy of honor, lady,
a man having died most nobly on behalf of Greece.[45]   310
Isn't this therefore shameful, if we use him as a friend while he's
looking at the light of day, but, when he's dead, we no longer
   do?[46]

---

45 The Homeric Achilles would be surprised to learn he died *pro patria*. The
Achilles reported in this drama seems even more self-centered than his
Iliadic predecessor; see Pantelis (2002) on how Achilles changes from
the *Iliad* in fifth-century tragedy.

46 The ideas of shame and honor here would be a particularly powerful
argument. Traditional Greek ethics were largely based on shame, an
externally validated criterion of praise and blame, which is contrasted
with guilt, whose source is internalized, though Cairns argues that we
overrate this distinction between shame and guilt. Honor also is not a
sense of internal self-worth, but the measure of one's standing in the
eyes of others. In Homer Achilles withdraws from the Trojan War over
a slight to his honor, and in Sophocles' *Ajax* the hero Ajax attempts to
kill his commanders and then commits suicide because of the sense
of humiliation after they award Achilles' armor to Odysseus. What
others would praise or censure played a large role in the decisions of
most ancient Greeks. In the fifth century B.C.E., Socrates' concern with
absolute standards of morality to which the individual would aspire,
regardless of the majority regarded as right, was revolutionary. The
Hecuba straddles these two worlds.

Well then. What will someone say, if ever there appears again
some mustering of the troops and some struggle with enemies?[47]
Will we fight, or will we be in love with our own lives,   315
seeing that the dead man is not honored?
And certainly, to me at least while I'm alive, if I should
have something small each day, it would be totally enough;
but my tomb I would want thought worthy
to be seen; for gratitude lasts a long time.[48]   320
       But if you claim you suffer pitiful things, listen
   to me in response:
there are among us old women and men
no less wretched than you,
and young brides bereft of their bridegrooms
whose bodies here the dust of Ida[49] hides.   325
Endure this. But as for us, if we think wrongly in
honoring a noble man, we will accept a charge of stupidity;
You barbarians[50] don't consider your friends friends,
nor do you hold in awe those who died nobly,
so that Greece may prosper,   330
while you receive what matches your designs.

CHORUS

Aiai. Slavery is always by nature bad
and it compels unnecessary suffering during violent conquest.[51]

HECUBA

Oh daughter, my words were thrown

---

47 Note the Polymestor later (1136-44) uses this same justification of a
    general future threat to kill Polydorus.
48 Gratitude is *kharis*. The context of the drama makes this assertion quite
    ironic, since most of the characters here show no sense of stable *kharis*
    and Odysseus is, as he speaks, proving himself ungrateful to Hecuba.
49 Mt. Ida, the most prominent feature of the landscape around Troy. Note
    also that the Chorus later will link the war-time suffering of women
    on both sides of the conflict, though certainly not to the same end as
    Odysseus suggests.
50 Euripidean drama frequently returns to theme of Greeks vs. barbarians,
    though often to question who is the real "barbarian." See Edith Hall's
    Inventing the Barbarian (1989) on the "discovery" of the Greek sense of
    superior "Greekness" after the Persian Wars early in the fifth century
    and its representation on the Athenian stage.
51 See the Interpretive Essay for my comments on slavery in Euripidean
    drama.

to the sky in vain concerning your murder;[52]   335
But you, if you have greater power than your mother,
make haste, hurling all your voices
like the mouth of a nightingale, that you not be deprived of life.
Fall pitifully at the knee of this Odysseus
and persuade him — you have the excuse; for even he has   340
children — that he should pity your lot.

POLYXENA

I see you, Odysseus, hiding your right hand
under your cloak and turning your face
back away, lest I reach out and touch your cheek.
Courage. You have escaped my prayer to Suppliant Zeus.[53]   345
Thus shall I submit both for the sake of necessity
and because I desire death.[54] But if I shall not want it,
I shall appear a base and life-loving woman.
Why then must I live? My father was once lord
of all the Phrygians; this was the first part of my life   350
when I was raised with lovely hopes
to be the bride of kings, with no small envy in my marriage,
whosoever's house and hearth I would approach.
And I was an ill-starred mistress to the women of Mt. Ida
and admired by wives and maidens,   355
equal to the gods save for death alone.
But now I am a slave. First, the very name, unaccustomed,
makes me love death;
then, the chance my lot would fall to masters
savage in their hearts, the kind who'd buy me for silver,   360
assigning the sister of Hector, and of many others,

---

52 Hecuba is careful to differentiate between true sacrifice to the gods and
   murder (*phonos*), as here.
53 The physical touching of the body is both an important part of
   supplication and a powerful gesture in the theater. The actor playing
   Odysseus clearly must be making a very visible effort to keep away from
   contact with Polyxena. Compare the importance of the Nurse's physical
   contact with Phaedra in *Hippolytus*. The cult designation Suppliant Zeus
   occurs elsewhere in tragedy at Aeschylus' *Suppliant Women* 616 and
   Sophocles' *Philoctetes* 484.
54 The text here plays off the Greek belief that a successful sacrifice depends
   upon the victim's consent to death which thus released the sacrificer
   from the pollution of murderous bloodshed.

to compulsory cooking in the house,
compelling me
to sweep the house and to stand at the loom,
passing the painful day;
and my bed — *my bed!*— a slave bought from some place   365
will touch, a bed once thought worthy of kings.
No! Never! From free eyes I release
this light, to Hades assigning my body.
So lead me, Odysseus, and, leading me, put an end to me.
For I see among us a courage neither from any hope nor
    expectation   370
that I must ever prosper again.
Mother, you, please don't get in my way,
whether with words or actions; share this desire with me
to die before something shameful or unworthy happens to us.
For whoever is not accustomed to taste troubles,   375
he endures, but aches placing the yoke on his neck.
He would be more fortunate dead
than alive; for a bad life is a great trial.

CHORUS
The stamp of noble men is awesome and visible
among mortals, and the name of noble birth   380
goes further for those worthy of it.

HECUBA
You have spoken well, daughter, but pain
goes with the good. But if there must be favor
for the son of Peleus and your side must escape
reproach, Odysseus, don't kill this girl,   385
But take me to the pyre of Achilles and
stab me — don't spare me. For I bore Paris,
who killed the son of Thetis,[55] striking him with his arrows.

ODYSSEUS
Not your death, old woman, did the phantom of Achilles
demand, but this girl's.   390

---

55 Achilles. Paris, whose seduction of Helen caused the Trojan War, killed
   Achilles with the help of Apollo while Achilles was trying to assault the
   walls of Troy.

HECUBA

So then murder me with my daughter
and twice as much blood will fall
for the earth and the corpse who demanded this![56]

ODYSSEUS

Your daughter's death is sufficient, and one death
must not be added to another; we don't owe yours.   395

HECUBA (*moves towards Polyxena and lays hold of her*)

There is great necessity for me to die with my daughter.

ODYSSEUS

How so? I didn't know I'd acquired a master.

HECUBA

Nonetheless, like ivy to oak, so will I cling to her.

ODYSSEUS

No, if at least you'd obey those wiser than you.

HECUBA

So I won't willingly release this child.   400

ODYSSEUS

But neither will I depart, leaving this child here.

POLYXENA

Mother, listen to me. And you, son of Laertes,
give some slack to my reasonably enraged parent,
and you, oh wretched woman, don't fight the powerful.
Do you want to be thrown down to the ground and
        scrape your   405
aged skin, violently shoved off,
torn away in public disgrace by a young man's arm,
the very things you will suffer? Don't let it happen to you.
        For it is not worthy.
But, oh my mother, give me your hand so sweet
and throw your cheek against mine.   410
Since never again, but just now I shall behold
the sun's final ray and circle.
Welcome the end of my speeches.
Oh mother who bore me, I depart now below.

---

56 Blood-offerings to the dead were poured on the ground and believed
   to be drunk by the dead.

HECUBA

Pitiful you are, child, but I am a wretched woman.   415

POLYXENA

There in Hades I shall lie apart from you.

HECUBA

Oh no. What should I do? Where shall I end my life?

POLYXENA

A slave I shall die, born from a free father.

HECUBA

Oh daughter, we will slave in the light.

POLYXENA

Unmarried, without wedding songs that were my rightful lot.

HECUBA

And we now have lost our share of fifty children.[57]

POLYXENA

What should I say for you to Hector and your aged
husband?   420

HECUBA

Announce that I am most wretched of all women.

POLYXENA

Oh bosom and breasts that gladly nursed me.

HECUBA

Oh daughter of a fate miserable and out of season.   425

POLYXENA

Farewell, mother, farewell from me also, Cassandra —

HECUBA

The others "fare well," but for your mother this isn't possible.[58]

POLYXENA

— and my brother Polydorus among the horse-loving Thracians.

HECUBA

If he really still lives; I am skeptical, as I am totally luckless.

---

57 Here, and elsewhere, Hecuba speaks of Cassandra, now a slave and
bedmate of Agamemnon, as if she were already dead.

58 Hecuba here plays off the two senses of the verb *khairein*, which, like
its English equivalent, signifies greetings and departures, as well as
pleasure in success.

POLYXENA

He lives and he will close your eyes in death.   430

HECUBA

I am dead before death because of troubles.

POLYXENA

Attend me now, Odysseus, and place my robes about my head[59]
since even before the sacrifice my heart is wasted
by mother's laments and I waste hers with mourning.
Oh light of day: since I can address your name,   435
No time remains with you save for how long I go
between the sword and the pyre of Achilles.

Odysseus leads Polyxena off to the camps at the right

HECUBA (*collapsing*)

Oh I. I faint. My limbs lie loose.
Oh my daughter. Touch mother, stretch out your hand.
Give. Don't leave me childless. I am lost, friends....   440
[If only I could see the Spartan woman, sister of the Dioscouroi,[60]
Helen. For through her lovely eyes
most shamefully did she bring Hell to Troy's happiness.[61]]

*Hecuba is left lying on the ground — perhaps in the middle of the orchestra
— while the chorus circles around her.*

First Choral Song

CHORUS   *strophe a*

Breeze, sea breeze,   445
since you attend the seafaring
swift skiffs against the sea swell,
to where will you send miserable me

---

59 As noted above, Polyxena must have carried some clothing into the
    acting area, which she now ask Odysseus to help her don, or she already
    wears a garment that allows her to be veiled. Given the importance
    attached during Talthybius' narrative to her more general disrobing,
    the intitial investiture must have occurred on stage, in order to load the
    later narrative with the memory of her garments. Veiling can visually
    mark approaching death or the status of a bride; see Oakley and Sinos
    (1993). Polyxena is subsequently cast as a Bride of Death, on the model
    of Persephone.

60 The Dioscouroi are Castor and Polydeuces.

61 This alludes to the "Helen ode" in the *Agamemnon* (681-90), continuing
    its pun on the stem *hel-*, which denotes destruction.

on my journey? At whose house as a bought
slave will I arrive?
to the haven in the Dorian land[62] ?   450
or in Phthia[63] where they say
the father of the finest waters,
Apidanos, makes fields fertile?
Or in the islands, miserably sent   *antistrophe b*
by the briny oar,   455
keeping a pitiful livelihood in the house,
where both the first-born palm
and the laurel extend their sacred
shoots for Leto,   460
a pleasing talisman for the birthpains from Zeus.[64]
With the Delian maidens
shall I praise the golden headband and bow
of divine Artemis?[65]   465
Or in the city of Pallas   *strophe b*
on the saffron robe
will I yoke the foals of Athena
with their lovely chariots on
cunningly wrought embroidery, [66]   470

---

62 "Dorian" was a name the Greeks gave to one of their two main linguistic
    and religious groupings (the other being Ionian). Their ancestor was
    said to be Heracles. Thucydides 1.2 holds that the Dorians were relative
    newcomers who conquered the Achaeans roughly eighty years after the
    fall of Troy. In the fifth century, Ionians were not welcome at the new
    Spartan colony of Heraclea, so the Athenians re-instituted the Ionian
    Festival of Delian Apollo (Thucydides 3.92), to which the *Hecuba* alludes
    in the succeeding antistrophe.
63 The homeland of Achilles.
64 The goddess Leto bore Artemis and Apollo for Zeus. Leto's difficulty
    giving birth to them is told in *The Homeric Hymn to Apollo*; in that poem
    Leto uses the palm and laurel to support herself while in labor (117).
65 The island of Delos is an important center of the worship of Artemis and
    Apollo. This passage alludes to the Dance of the Maidens at the Delian
    Festival of Apollo, which may have just recently been restored by the
    Athenians (Thucydides 3.104).
66 This alludes to the robe woven for Athena at the Panathenaiac Festival
    in Athens, whose climax was a presentation of this robe at the statue of
    Athena Polias. The chorus members thus imagine themselves as inhabitants
    of Athens, practicing the same rituals as the members of the audience, but,
    as slaves and foreigners, they would be excluded from the weaving of the
    robe. Even their happier possible lives are marked by delusion.

bright woven saffron threads, or
the race of Titans[67]
which Zeus son of Kronos
puts into deepest sleep
with fires flaming about?

Oh my children,   *antistrophe b*   475
Oh my fathers and my land,
which falls to ruins in smoke,
smouldering, spear-won
by the Argives; but I in a foreign
land am called   480
slave, having left Asia,
homes in Europe traded for
bedrooms in Hades.

The Chorus perhaps stops moving at a place that conceals Hecuba, who still
lies prostrate on the ground from her collapse at 438-40. Talthybius enters,
unannounced, from the camp at the right. His entrance may have been visible
throughout much of the ode, since he is unlikely to have been moving with
much haste due to the message he is bringing Hecuba.[68]

TALTHYBIUS
Where, you Trojan girls, can I find her who once was
queen of Ilium, Hecuba?   485

CHORUS
Here she is lying near you, with her back on the ground,
Talthybius, wrapped up in her robes.[69]

---

67 This refers to the Titans' younger brothers, the Giants. The battle of the
    Olympians against the Giants, called the Gigantomachy, was a popular
    subject in art; on the Gigantomachy, see Apollodorus, *The Library of Greek*
    Mythology 1.6.1-2.

68 I speculate that the Chorus blocks the view of Talthybius because he
    needs to ask about Hecuba's whereabouts. There are other instances,
    for example, *Heracles* 1189, where a speaker fails to recognize a veiled
    character, but Talthybius does not seem to see any character at all.

69 If the Chorus surrounds or simply stands between Talthybius and
    Hecuba, then it steps back back her to allow him to see her. Hecuba has
    mirrored her daughter's veiling by covering her head, but Hecuba's
    action signals mourning, not marriage (however ironic). Both gestures
    mark Polyxena's passage to death and foreshadow the entrance of the
    covered corpse of Polydorus.

TALTHYBIUS

Oh Zeus, what should I say? that you are watching humans
or that you have acquired this reputation in vain,
[and we, falsely, believe there is a race of gods,]   490
and that chance oversees all things among mortals?[70]
Was this not the queen of the Phrygians rich in gold,
was this not the wife of Priam rich in blessings?
And now her entire city is razed by the spear,
and she herself a slave, aged, childless, upon the ground   495
lies, defiling with dirt her wretched head.
Woe, woe! I am an old man, but still may I die
before falling to some shameful chance.
            Get up, unhappy one, and lift further
and raise your side and snow-white head.   500

*Talthybius has moved to Hecuba's side during his speech and finally crouched
down to help her up.*

HECUBA

Let me be. Who is this who does not let my body
lie? Why do you disturb me in my grief, whoever you are?

TALTHYBIUS

I am Talthybius. I have come to do the work of the Danaans.
Agamemnon sent me, lady.

HECUBA

Dearest man! Have you come to announce it seems best
to the Achaeans to add me to the sacrifice at the tomb?   505
How then you would say things friendly to me! Come on,
let's hurry up. Lead me on, old man!

TALTHYBIUS

Your girl is gone, lady, and I've come after you so
that you bury her. Both the
two Atreids[71] and the Achaean people send me.   510

HECUBA

Oh no! What will you say? You haven't really come for us

---

70 At 491 and again at 498, Talthybius evokes *tuchê*, chance, an important
    theme in a play where its characters fortunes suffer such violent reversals
    (which were echoed in the contemporaneous experience of the audience).
    See my note on line 786.
71 The two sons of Atreus, Agamemnon and Menelaus.

so we can die, but to signal troubles?
Dead you are, Oh child, ripped from your mother!
We are childless after you. Oh wretched me.
How did you make an end of her? Did you show her proper
    respect?   515
Or did you approach the terrible deed by killing her as an
enemy, old man? Speak, even if you'll say unwelcome things.

TALTHYBIUS
Double are the tears you require me to reap, lady,
in pity of your daughter; for both now by speaking her troubles[72]
I will wet this eye and so I did before when she died by the
    grave.   520
The whole mob[73] from the Achaean army was present
by the tomb for the sacrifice of your girl.
The son of Achilles took Polyxena by the hand
and stood her upon the mound's top. I was nearby.
The young men chosen from the Achaeans were gathered   525
to restrain the bucking of your calf[74] and
followed behind. Taking in his hands a full cup
all of gold, the son of Achilles raises with one hand
libations to his dead father. To me he signals
to herald silence to the whole army of the Achaeans.   530
And I posititioned myself in their midst and said:

---

72 Messenger-speeches in Greek tragedy typically narrate events that
    cannot be enacted on stage because they require a substantial change of
    scene, a large crowd and bloodshed. Messengers in Euripidean drama
    never report the events they witness in neutral terms; see de Jong (1991),
    63-79.
73 Gregory points out here that context should determine whether the
    Greek word *okhlos* is pejorative in the English sense of "mob" (605, 607,
    868) or the more neutral "crowd" (521, 533). But I think that we need
    to retain the same English term for both, as the audience would hear
    the same Greek word in each place and consider how a crowd becomes
    a mob. This drama does offer a telling study of mob psychology as it
    depicts the wildly fluctuating responses of the crowd during the debate
    over human sacrifice, their rapid shifts in response to Polyxena herself,
    and the conversion of the suffering group of Trojan women into a gang
    willing to kill children. This mutability leads Hecuba to order the *okhlos*
    to be kept from Polyxena's corpse.
74 This language reminds all that Polyxena is being substituted for a normal
    sacrificial animal in an action that should produce a communal meal.

"Silence, Achaeans, may the whole people be quiet,
Silence, quiet." And I made the mob calm down.
And he said: *"Oh son of Peleus, my father,*
receive from me these libations of appeasement,   535
summoners of corpses. Come, so you may drink the dark
pure blood of a girl, which to you we present as a gift,
the army and I. Become favorable to us
and grant release to the prows and moorings
of our ships and grant us all to   540
happen upon a gentle homecoming to the fatherland."
So many things he spoke, and all the army joined in prayer.
Then he took hold of a gold-crusted knife,[75]
dragging it from its scabbard, and he nodded to the young men
picked from the army of the Argives to grab the virgin.   545
And she, as she considered the situation, made this speech:
"Oh Argives who sacked my city of Troy,
I consent to death. Let nobody touch my skin.
I will offer my neck firm in resolve.
By the gods, let me go and kill me   550
free, so I may die free; for among the dead
I feel shame to be called slave though I am royalty."[76]
The people roared their approval, and lord Agamemnon
said to the youths to release the virgin.
[And they released her, as soon as they heard   555
the last word, from him whose power is greatest.]
And when she heard this command of her masters
she grabbed hold of her robes from her highest shoulder
and tore them down almost to her hips,

---

75 A gold cup for the wine and a gold knife for the sacrifice contrast sharply
   with and thus comment on the squalid existence Polyxena now escapes.
   And were these trinkets acquired from the royal house of Hecuba in
   Troy?

76 In Greek sacrificial practice, the staging of the victim's consent to be
   sacrificed was critical in absolving the sacrificers of guilt; see Burkert
   (1985) 55-58. Euripides here likely wants his audience to remember that
   Agamemnon has already seen a virgin sacrifice before the war, but of his
   daughter Iphigenia; in Aeschylus' *Agamemnon* the Chorus remembers
   how Agamemnon gagged his daughter before she could curse him, let
   alone make a speech.

and revealed her breasts and bosom,[77]   560
as beautiful as those of a statue, and dropping
her knee to the earth she spoke the boldest speech of all:
"Look right here, young man, if you are eager
to strike my chest, strike here, but if it's under the neck
you want, then this throat is here and ready."   565
And he both willing and unwilling by pity of the girl,
cuts with his blade the pipes of her breath;
her life streamed away. But she even in death still
planned carefully ahead and fell with propriety,
hiding what one must from the eyes of males.[78]   570
And after she let go her breath in fatal slaughter
all of the Argives took up different tasks;
some from their hands threw leaves
on the dead girl,[79] while others were building the pyre by
bringing pine logs. But anyone slacking off   575
heard such abuse from another who wasn't:
"Are you just standing there, you miscreant, holding
in hand neither robe nor adornment for the young lady?
Aren't you going to give something to her who was
so great in resolve and best in spirit?" In saying such things   580
about your dead daughter, I see you are of all women
best in children and worst in luck.

77 Polyxena clearly has no erotic intent in this action. The baring of breasts by older women can suggest mourning, as in the case of Hecuba's desperate gesture to Hector while he flees from Achilles (*Iliad* 22.80-83) or an attempt to appeal to the early maternal bond, as when Clytemnestra tries to stop Orestes from killing her (Aeschylus, *Libation Bearers* 868-98). Such situations, of course, do not apply to Polyxena. Scodel (1996) 125 argues that the gesture controls the exposure of her body and thus affirms her freedom. Thalmann (1993) 146 posits a ritual significance to the action, wherein the signs of her former self are shed in a rite of passage. However, while her intention is not erotic, her gesture does have an erotic effect on her audience.

78 The tone of this episode oscillates between the nobility of Polyxena's gesture, and the voyeurism attached to the description of her nudity. Both here and in Hecuba's later fears there is unmistakable reference to the effect of her visible sexuality on the army.

79 The showering of leaves was a form of congratulation to victorious athletes in the Olympics.

CHORUS

Some awesome sorrow is this which boiled over on Priam's
    daughters
and on my city by the compulsions of the gods.

HECUBA

Oh daughter, I know not what part of troubles I shall look to   585
when there are so many present. For if I should touch one,
this one here doesn't let me go, and then some other grief
calls me aside in succession of troubles on troubles.
And now I could not wash from my mind
your suffering so as not to mourn you;   590
but now you've really removed the excess in the reports
of your nobility. Isn't it amazing, that if some bad soil
gets some timely luck from the gods it bears corn well,
but good soil, if it misses the things it needs,
then it gives a bad harvest? But among men always   595
the wicked is nothing else than bad,
and the good is always good, and because of disaster
he does not corrupt his nature but is always good?[80]
[Do parents make the difference, or education?
Still, also a good upbringing   600
teaches what is right; if someone should learn this well,
he knows the shameful, having learned it by the yardstick of the
    good.]
And yet a mind shoots forth these things in vain like arrows;
(to Talthybius) but you go and tell this to the Argives:
let nobody touch her, as far as I'm concerned, but keep the
    mob away   605
from my girl. In a large army
the mob is insatiable and the anarchy of sailors is
stronger than fire, and the man not doing anything evil is tagged
    evil himself.
(to serving woman) And you then take an urn, my old handmaid,
dip it in the salty sea and bring it here,   610
so that I may give my child her final bath,

---

80 These lines are central to Nussbaum's meditation (1986) 397-421 on the
    relationship between nature and nurture in this tragedy.

the unmarried bride, the virgin no-virgin,[81]
and I might lay her out — how worthily? from where?
I couldn't! But as I am able (for what would I suffer?)
collecting a gown from the spear-won women,   615
who sitting by me dwell inside these tents,
perhaps one has slipped by her new masters
some theft from her own home.
   Oh image of my house, Oh once blessed homes,
Oh you richest, blessed above all in children,   620
Priam, here am I the aged mother of your children;
thus we have come to nothing, stripped of our
earlier spirit. And then do we puff ourselves up,
one of us because of his wealthy houses,
another because he is called "honored among citizens"?   625
These things are nothing, the vain plans of minds
and boasts of the tongue. That man is most blessed,
to whom each day nothing bad happens.

Hecuba and attendants re-enter the skênê; *Talthybius exits to the right, the
serving woman to left.*[82]

Second Choral Song
CHORUS   *strophe*
For me disaster was necessary,
for me pain was necessary,   630
from that moment when first Alexander[83] cut the pine
forest of Mt. Ida, to launch his sea voyage
for the bed of Helen, whom gold-gleaming   635
Helios illuminates

---

81 Following the pattern of the virgin Persephone who married Hades
   himself, girls who died before their weddings were thought to have
   married Death. See Seaford (1987).
82 Euripides has now motivated, in terms of the plot construction, the connection between the deaths of the two children, for as soon as Hecuba
   dispatches the Serving Maid to the seashore for Polyxena's bath water,
   Euripides begins to escalate the tension over Hecuba's discovery of the
   death of her son.
83 Paris. Mt. Ida was where the infant Paris was exposed after it was
   prophesied that he would destroy Troy. He was suckled by a bear and
   eventually found by a shepherd, and thus Paris spent his youth on
   the slopes of Mt. Ida. See Apollodorus, *The Library of Greek Mythology*
   3.12.5

as most beautiful.

Labors and compulsions[84] stronger than	*antistrophe*
labors come circling around,	640

a common trouble from a private
idiocy,[85] deadly upon the land of Simois,
and disaster came to the others.

Strife was judged, on Ida	
a shepherd man judges	645

the three daughters of the blessed ones,[86]

leading to the spear and murder and outrage of my	
chambers;	*epode*
Some Spartan girl, with many tears at home	650

also groans around fair-flowing Eurotas,[87]
and upon her own grey head the mother of
dead children

sets her hand, claws her cheek,	655

setting her bloody nails for mangling.[88]

SERVING MAID (*entering from left, accompanied by at least two mute extras carrying a covered body into the orchestra*)[89]

Women, where is all-suffering Hecuba,
who is victorious over every man and woman in a contest

---

84 *Anankê*, here "compulsion" or "necessity" continues the theme of necessity, real and apparent, which circulates throughout the drama. See Interpretive Essay.

85 Literally, "from a private folly." Our word "idiot" is derived from the Greek *idios*, which merely means "private." Simois was one of the two rivers of Troy.

86 Strife (*Eris*) was the goddess who, after not being invited to the wedding of Peleus and Thetis, threw the golden apple among Hera, Athena and Aphrodite, to make them quarrel over who was fairest. Zeus sent them with Hermes to Paris on Mt. Ida. Strife thus caused strife. Apollodorus, *The Library of Greek Mythology* 3.12.3.

87 Eurotas is the main river of Sparta.

88 The reference to Sparta here connects the homeland of Menelaus and Helen with the city that is fighting Athens at the time of the *Hecuba*'s production.

89 The audience is likely here in suspense as to which corpse will be brought back first, the son's or the daughter's; since Talthybius has been directed to secure Polyxena's corpse, the greater expectation might be for her. As soon as the cortege becomes visible at the left, it knows that was wrong. Note also the recurring motif of covering, begun by Polyxena and continued by Hecuba.

of troubles? None will take her crown prize away.[90]   660

CHORUS

What is it, you wretched person, with your cries of bad tidings?
How these painful announcements never seem to rest.

SERVING MAID

To Hecuba I bring this pain: amidst troubles
it's not at all easy for mortals to speak auspiciously.

CHORUS

She happens now to be passing through the house.   665
Look, she appears at the sound of your words.

(Hecuba appears at the skênê *door and enters the acting area)*

SERVING MAID

Oh, all-wretched and still more so than I can speak,
queen, you're dead, you no longer exist, though still you behold
     the sun's light,
childless, husbandless, stateless, destroyed.

HECUBA

You spoke nothing new, hurling abuse at those already
     aware,   670
But why have you come to me attending
this corpse of Polyxena , whose burial was announced
as the earnest work of all the Achaeans?[91]

SERVING MAID

This woman knows nothing, but, I think, she laments
Polyxena, and doesn't grasp her new woes.   675

HECUBA

Not again! Surely you don't bear here
the Bacchic head of the prophet Cassandra?

SERVING MAID (*unveiling the corpse as she speaks*)

You lament the living girl, but the dead boy here you don't yet
mourn; so gaze upon the bared body of the corpse,
see if some astonishment appears to you, even beyond
     expectation.   680

---

90 The servant here imagines a contest of suffering in the Olympic Games,
    to be rewarded, as with other events, with a laurel crown of victory.
91 The audience, having seen the entrances from the left, knows that this
    corpse cannot be Polyxena's, as she had exited to the right. Hecuba,
    however, lacks this knowledge because she had been inside.

HECUBA

Oimoi. I see a boy, my boy, dead,
Polydorus, whom a Thracian man was keeping safe in his house
    for me!
I am finished, lost, I no longer exist!

(Hecuba breaks into irregular, sung, lyrics, while the others remain in iambic speech)

Oh child, child,
aiai, I begin my Bacchic song   685
from a god of Vengeance,[92]
in late-learning of my troubles.[93]

SERVING MAID

Did you, unhappy woman, recognize your son's disaster?

HECUBA

Unbelievable, unbelievable, new new things I weep!
Troubles after troubles meet troubles.   690
Never will a day without groans and tears
hold me!

CHORUS

Terrible, Oh sad one, terrible troubles we suffer.

HECUBA

Oh child child of an unhappy mother
by what lot are you dead? by what fate do you lie there?   695
by the hand of what human being?

SERVING MAID

I don't know. I found him at the seashore...

HECUBA

Thrown out, on the smooth sand,
or felled by a bloody spear?   700

---

92 The text is disputed here. I generally keep Diggle's reading, but move
    the comma to after *alastoros* (vengeance) because Polydorus' death as an
    act of vengeance makes little sense. Hecuba here begins to plot revenge,
    and Bacchic imagery in this drama is associated with vengeance.

93 Late-learning is a common theme in Greek tragedy as characters learn
    late, usually too late, the truth about themselves and their situation. One
    thinks here, for example of Theseus and Hippolytus in Euripides' *Hip-
    polytus,* or Deianira and Heracles in Sophocles' *Trachiniae,* two dramas
    produced within a few years of the *Hecuba.*

SERVING MAID

An ocean wave bore him from the sea.

HECUBA

Oh no! *Aiai.* I understand the sleepy vision
of my eyes, (no dark-winged ghost
passed by me), the vision I saw about you,   705
Oh child, that you no longer lived in Zeus' light.

CHORUS

Who killed him then? Can you say by interpreting dreams?

HECUBA

My, my, guest-friend, the Thracian horseman,   710
where his old father had placed him in hiding.

CHORUS

Oh no. What will you say? He killed him to get the gold?

HECUBA

Unspeakable, unnamable, beyond wonders,
unholy and unbearable. Where is the justice of guest-friends? 715
Oh most damnable of men, how you butchered his
flesh, cutting with an iron knife
his limbs — you did not pity this boy.[94] ← *torture? Cut apart to hide?* 720

CHORUS

Oh suffering one, how the divinity that made you
most-suffering among mortals is heavy on you.
But I see the shape of the master here,
Agamemnon, so let's be silent, friends.   725

(Agamemnon enters from right)

AGAMEMNON

Hecuba, why do you delay coming to cover your child
in a grave, especially since Talthybius gave me your order
that none of the Argives touch your daughter?
We let you have your way and didn't touch her;[95]
but you are dawdling so much that I'm amazed.   730

---

94 The knife marks could suggest some kind of ritual mutilation of the
    body by Polymestor. In any case, the extent of the trauma to the corpse
    indicates Polymestor did not simply stab Polydorus and kill him.
95 The Greek could mean "we left her alone", but Agamemnon does seem
    to be complaining about the lack of follow-through from Hecuba after
    her specific demands were made.

I have come to fetch you, for matters have been
handled well there, if any of these matters could be "well".
Wait. What man do I see here at the tent,
one of the Trojan dead? For the robes enfolding
his corpse tell me he's not Argive.   735

HECUBA

(*turning aside*) Miserable one! — For I address myself addressing
    you — [96]
Hecuba, what should I do? Throw myself at the knees
of Agamemnon here or bear my troubles in silence?

AGAMEMNON

Why, turning your back to my face,
do you weep? Won't you say what's been done? Who is this
    here?[97]   740

HECUBA (*still talking to herself*)

But, if, considering me a slave and hostile,
    he should shove me from his knees, we'd be put to more pain.

AGAMEMNON

I am not a prophet by nature, so that, without hearing,
I'd still learn the path of your plans.

HECUBA (*still talking to herself*)

Do I then calculate his mind to be more hostile   745
when he really isn't hostile?

AGAMEMNON

If you wish me to know none of this,
you've reached the same place as me. For I also do not wish to
    hear.

---

96 A very self-conscious phrase, but Euripides needs to signal to his
audience that Hecuba is talking to herself, not a terribly common event
in the Athenian theater; cf Medea when she deliberates killing her own
children.

97 A masked actor performing in a large outdoor theater cannot communicate tears by shedding false ones. The actor who performs Hecuba must
be engaging in large gestures to communicate weeping.

HECUBA

Without this man I would not be able to avenge
my children.[98] Why do I keep turning these things over?   750
Daring is necessary, whether I am lucky or not —

*(She turns to Agamemnon and sinks to her knees in supplication, grabbing
his legs with one hand and reaching up with the other)*

Agamemnon, I beseech you by your knees here
and by your cheek, and your blessed right hand...

AGAMEMNON

Seeking what matter? Is it to make your
life free? That's fairly easy.[99]   755

HECUBA

No, not at all. With vengeance exacted on the wicked
I would willingly spend my whole life in slavery.
It's nothing at all you might guess, my lord. —

AGAMEMNON

And for what assistance, then, do you call us?

HECUBA

Do you see the corpse here over which I weep?   760

AGAMEMNON

I see. But I can't understand what's coming next.

HECUBA

I brought this one to life once and I carried him inside me.

AGAMEMNON

But which of your children is this one, you wretched woman?

HECUBA

He's not one of the sons of Priam dead under Ilium.

---

98 The family of a murder victim was legally obliged to move against
the murderer; see MacDowell (1978) 109-11. Thus, as Mossman (1992)
180 observes, the audience would view retribution as the inevitable
consequence of this discovery. The reference to "children" and not just
"child" suggests she views her response as directed to Polyxena as well
as to Polydorus.

99 Euripides quickly establishes the moral vapidity of Agamemnon with
this trifling comment about slavery, which jars so strongly against the
hardships of slavery established throughout the earlier parts of the
drama.

AGAMEMNON

Well, did you then give birth to another one than them?   765

HECUBA

Yes, and with little profit, it seems, I bore the one you see here.

AGAMEMNON

Where did he happen to be when the city was destroyed?

HECUBA

His father sent him away, fearful of his death.

AGAMEMNON

To where then did he remove him alone from his other sons?

HECUBA

Into this land, the very place where he was discovered dead.   770

AGAMEMNON

To the man, Polymestor, who rules this land?

HECUBA

Here he was sent as the guardian of that most bitter gold.

AGAMEMNON

And at whose hands or by what fate is he dead?

HECUBA

Who else? The Thracian guest-friend killed him.

AGAMEMNON

Oh wretch.[100] And I suppose he lusted to seize the gold?   775

HECUBA

Exactly, when he recognized the disaster of the Phrygians.

AGAMEMNON

But where did you find him? Or did someone bring the corpse to you?

HECUBA (*gesturing to her serving maid*)

This woman did, stumbling upon it at the seashore.

AGAMEMNON

Was she looking for it, or working at some other task?

HECUBA

She went to bring some bathwater from the sea for Polyxena. 780

---

100 It is unclear whether the Greek indicates Polydorus, Polymestor or Hecuba.

AGAMEMNON
The guest-friend killed him, it seems, and threw him out.
HECUBA
Buffeted by the sea, his flesh hacked through.
AGAMEMNON
Oh your sadness of unmeasured hardships!
HECUBA
I am lost. No trouble still remains.
AGAMEMNON
Alas, alas! What woman was born so unfortunate?   785
HECUBA
None. Unless you mean Fortune herself.[101]
But listen why I fall at your knees.
If I seem to you to suffer things lawful to the gods,
then I would accept them. But if the opposite, then may you become
an avenger for me against the man, the most sacrilegious guest-
friend   790
who, fearing neither those below the earth, nor those above[102]
has done the most sacrilegious act,
[he who often shared my dinner table,
holding the first rank of hospitality[103] among my friends,
and though he received such things as are required, with forethought   795
he committed murder. And if he wanted to kill him, he didn't even deem
him worthy of a grave, but cast him out to the sea.]
While we may be slaves and without strength,
the gods still are strong and their ruler is

---

101 *Tuchê.* This is the personification of luck that Oedipus ironically posits
as his parent (*Oedipus Tyrannos* 1080) just before the truth of his birth is
revealed. *Tuchê* does not imply good or bad fortune, but rather simply
"what happens," or "chance." In order to preserve the repetition from
Hecuba's *dustuchês* (unfortunate) to Agamemnon's *Tuchê* (fortune), I
had to use an English term with a more positive connotation than the
Greek.
102 That is, the chthonic gods and the Olympians.
103 "Hospitality" here is *xenia*.

Law. We believe the gods exist by reason of law[104]   800
and we live with clear distinctions between unjust and just.
If law, having returned to your hands, will be destroyed,
and if whoever kills their guests does not pay,
or dares to carry off the sacred things of the gods,
fairness is not possible among men.   805
Therefore, counting these things among the shameful, have
    reverence for me:
Pity me, and having stepped back like a painter,
behold me and examine such troubles as I have.
I once was queen, but now I am your slave,
once lucky in children, now I am at once old and childless,   810
cityless, alone, most wretched of mortals....

*(Agamemnon turns away and breaks physical contact. Hecuba thus rises to
her feet in response)*

Ah miserable me, where do you turn your feet away
    from me?
It seems I'll do nothing now; Oh how miserable I am!
Why then do we mortals labor and pursue   815
other studies as if they're all necessary,
but we do not work to fulfill our understanding of
Persuasion,[105] the sole ruler of mankind,
by giving it money in payment, so that it would then be possible
to persuade and acquire at once whatever one wished?

---

104 The word translated as "law" twice here can mean "law" or "custom."
     In either case it denotes some guiding principle. What, exactly, this
     phrase "reason of law" means is disputed, but its import is crucial,
     since the distinction between nature (*physis*) and custom (*nomos*), and
     the question of whether human values come from one or the other,
     is fundamental to the intellectual and moral crises of the second half
     of the fifth century. Hecuba could mean "we believe in the gods by
     convention," as Nussbaum (1986) 400 argues. Gregory 1999 and Kovacs
     (1987) 101 maintain, on the other hand, that Hecuba would be foolish
     to argue that a villain should be punished on the basis of a universe
     governed by conventions, not absolutes. Further, Hecuba elsewhere
     advocates traditional views of the gods. Much of how one understands
     the play can come down to these lines.
105 Persuasion, *Peithô*, is personified as a goddess throught Greek tragedy,
     and is especially visible as a problem in Aeschylus' *Oresteia*. Buxton
     (1982) 32-36 observes that the goddess Peitho was worshipped in cult
     in Athens.

How, therefore, could one still hope to succeed?   820
For those who once were my sons no longer exist,
and myself I am driven by the spear to shameful acts,
and I see the smoke here leaping out over the city.
And yet — perhaps this is a stranger to my argument,
to toss in Aphrodite; but still it will be said:—   825
by your side my daughter lies,
the seer of Phoebus,[106] whom the Phrygians call Cassandra.
Where will you tally your pleasurable nights then, lord,
or for those passionate embraces in the bed
what thanks will my daughter have? and I for her?[107]   830
[both from the shadow and from the love-charms
of night arises the greatest joy to mortals.]
Listen then now: this dead one here — do you see him?
By treating this one well you'll do a favor for your
brother-in-law.[108] My speech still lacks one part.   835
If only voice were in my arms
and hands and hair and the step of my feet,
whether by the arts of Daedalus[109] or some god,
that all together they might grasp your knees,
weeping, bringing all sorts of prosecution speeches.   840
Oh master, Oh greatest light to the Greeks,
be persuaded, extend to an old woman a hand of
vengeance, even if it's nothing, still do it!
For it is the mark of a noble man both to serve justice
and everywhere always to treat badly the bad.   845

CHORUS
Remarkable how everything happens to mortals,
and the laws of necessity[110] demarcate them,

---

106 Apollo.
107 Note the return of appeals to the codes of reciprocity (*kharis*).
108 Polydorus, who is, of course, neither alive nor really a brother-in-law.
109 The legendary Athenian artisan who created, among other things, the
    device that allowed Pasiphae to mate with a bull and the wings with
    which he and his son Icarus tried to escape from Crete.
110 "The laws of necessity" (*nomoi anankês*) is a remarkable expression since
    anankê was so often personified as an absolute force outside of and indif-
    ferent to human reason and civilization.

placing the most bitter enemies in friendship
and putting in enmity those previously friendly.

AGAMEMNON

With pity I hold you and your son and your fortunes,   850
Hecuba, and your suppliant hand,
and, on account of the gods and justice
I wish the unholy guest-friend to pay this price of justice,
if only somehow it might both appear that I am favorable to you
and I would not seem to the army for Cassandra's sake   855
to plan this murder for the lord of Thrace.
For there is a matter where confusion has fallen on me:
this man the army considers an ally,
and the dead one their enemy; but if this one here is kin to me,
then this matter is separate and is none of the army's
business.   860
Think these things over; since, on the one hand, you have me
willing
to work with you and provide swift help,
but on the other, I'm slow, if suspected by the Achaeans.

HECUBA

(Deeply sighing)[111]
There is nobody among mortals who is free;
for either he is a slave of money or chance,   865
or the city's populace or written law[112]
keep him from using his character according to his judgment.
But since you are in fear and allot more weight to the mob,
I myself shall make you free of this fear.
For understand, first, that, if I should plot some trouble   870
for the murderer of this man here, you would not be an accomplice.
Next, if some uproar or defense appears from the Achaeans
on behalf of a suffering Thracian man, for such things he will
suffer,
keep them away, while still not appearing to do me a favor.
But as for the rest, don't worry, I'll take care of it nicely.   875

AGAMEMNON

But how? What will you do? Will you take a blade in your
old hand and kill the barbarian man,
or do it with poisons or by some other means?
What band of men will you have? Where will you get allies?[113]

HECUBA

These tents here conceal a mob of Trojan women.   880

AGAMEMNON

You mean the spear-prizes? the prey of the Greeks?

HECUBA

With these women I shall take vengeance on the murderer of
mine.

AGAMEMNON

And just how will women acquire power over men?

HECUBA

Terrible is their number, and, with deceit, hardly beatable.

AGAMEMNON

Terrible indeed. Yet still I find fault with feminine force.   885

HECUBA

But why? Did not women take down the sons of Aegyptus
and utterly empty Lemnos of men?[114]
But so let it be! Let go this argument,
then send this woman here safely for me through the army.
And you (*turning to the serving maid*), approach the Thracian
guest-friend,

---

113 Euripides here begins to prepare his audience to expect Hecuba to
murder Polymestor, so that her mutilation of his eyes should come as a
surprise.

114 These stories are the two most common paradigms for group female
violence against men. Aegyptus was feuding with his brother Danaos
over the throne of Egypt. The former had fifty sons and the latter as
many daughters. Eventually, marriages were arranged among all of the
children, but Danaos persuaded his daughters to kill their new husbands
on their wedding night. Only one, Hypermnestra, spared her husband.
The women then fled to Argos as suppliants. Aeschylus composed a
trilogy on this subject, whose last part, *Suppliant Women*, still survives.
The Lemnian Women were punished with a foul odor for their failure to
honor Aphrodite, and so their husbands refused to sleep with them. In
response, the women murdered their husbands, and they lived without
men until the Argonauts arrived.

and say: *"Hecuba the former queen of Ilium invites you,*
on a need no less yours than hers. Your sons too,
since the children also must hear the words from
her." — Agamemnon, you hold back on the burial
of freshly slaughtered Polyxena,   895
so that the sibling pair, a double anguish to their mother,
may lie close by in a single flame, and then be covered in the
earth.

AGAMEMNON
These things will be so. And yet if the army could
set sail, I could not grant this favor to you.
But now, since god releases no fair breezes,   900
they must remain watching for calm sailing.[115]
May it turn out well somehow, for this matter is common to all,
both to each private citizen and to the city,
that the bad suffer badly, and the good succeed.

Agamemnon leaves to right, the servant, to left. Hecuba remains; possibly
collapsing, if keimenê *("lying") in line 969 is to be taken literally*

Third Choral Song
CHORUS
You, Oh fatherland Ilium,   *strophe a*   905
will no longer be counted among the unsacked cities;
such a cloud of Greeks conceals you,
sacking you spear by spear,
your crown of towers hacked off,
stained in defilement with the most miserable smoke,   910
wretched city,
no longer will I set foot in you.
At midnight I was lost,   *antistrophe a*
when after feasts sweet sleep upon my eyes   915
was spread, and retiring from the dances and songful
offerings, he lay down,
my husband, in our bedchambers,

---

115 This observation complicates the earlier accounts of why the fleet cannot
     leave. As Gregory notes here, Greek usage would not allow for Achilles
     to be called a god (*theos*), so either the belief in divine agency here is a
     sham, or the gods are working in more mysterious ways. On the winds
     and the gods, see Gregory (1999) xxix-xxxi, Thalmann (1993) 153-54 and
     Mitchell-Boyask (1993) 116-19.

his spearshaft in its holder,
no longer watching   920
for a naval brigade
that had trod Ilium's Troy.
I was arranging my hair,   *strophe b*
bound up with nets,
beholding my golden mirrors'   925
limitless gleamings,
so I might fall into bed.
But clamor came through the city;
And this was the order down through
Troy's town: "You
sons of Greeks, when, when
after sacking the summit of Ilium   930
will you come to your own homes?"
Abandoning my bed,   *antistrophe b*
barely clothed, like a Dorian maiden,[116]
clinging to august Artemis,[117]
I, wretch, achieved nothing.   935
But, having seen my bedmate dead,
I am led upon the salty sea,
looking away back to the city, when
the ship moved my foot from
homecoming   940
and split me
from the land of Ilium;
miserable, I collapsed in pain.
The sister of the Dioscouroi,[118] Helen,   *epode*
and the herdsman of Ida,
baneful Paris,   945
I curse them both,
since their marriage blasted me

116 Herodotus 5.88.1 indicates that Dorian was a standard term attached to
     the clothing *peplos* which all Greek women once wore.
117 Artemis, the virgin goddess of the hunt who was a special figure in cult
     for unmarried girls. The Chorus here probably is imagining clinging to
     a statue of Artemis for protection.
118 Castor and Polydeuces, whose other sister, Clytemnestra, is mentioned
     in Polymestor's prophecies at the end.

from my ancestral land
and made me homeless — no, not marriage
but some misery from a spirit of vengeance.
May the salt sea not return her home again   950
nor may she reach
her father's house.

Polymestor enters from left, accompanied by sons and bodyguards, and Hecuba's servant.

POLYMESTOR
Oh Priam most beloved of men, and you most beloved,
Hecuba, I weep beholding you and your city
and your offspring who died just now.[119]   955
Alas.
Nothing can be trusted, neither good reputation
nor that one who succeeds won't then fail.
And the gods themselves disturb things back and forth,
establishing confusion, so that by ignorance
we worship them.[120] But why must one   960
lament these matters and make no progress before troubles?
Yet you, if you at all would reproach my absence,
please hold off; for I happened to be away in the midst of
the borders of Thrace, when you came here. And then after I'd
    arrived home,
I barely set foot outside my house when   965
this slavewoman of yours here fell into the same place,
speaking words, which, when I heard, I came.

HECUBA (*keeping her face turned from Polymestor*)
I am ashamed to look you in the eye,

---

119 This sequence should indicate that the shrouded corpse of Polydorus
    is still present, and Polymestor, like Hecuba earlier, mistakes it for
    Polyxena. Kovacs, however, argues that the body was removed at the
    close of the previous scene, but, in my view, there are no clear signs of
    removal, and the corpse' presence is vital to the action of this scene.

120 These remarks might clarify the earlier ambiguities in Hecuba's speech
    whether we believe in the gods by convention or the gods rule by
    law. Polymestor's actions characterize a godless man and his words
    here about the gods more openly advance a skeptical view of divine
    agency than in Hecuba's speech, which thus seems designed to balance
    Polymestor's here.

Polymestor, while lying here in such troubles.
To be seen by someone who knew me when prosperous,
    shame[121] holds me   970
that I happen to be in this lot where I am now,
and I would not be able to look at you right in the eyes.
Please don't consider it hostility to you,
[Polymestor; besides, custom is somewhat responsible,
that women don't behold men face-to-face.]   975

POLYMESTOR
And it's no wonder at all! But what need do you have of me?
On what matter did you send my foot from my house?

HECUBA
A private matter of my own do I want to speak to you
and your sons; order your attendants (for my sake)
to stand back from this house here.   980

POLYMESTOR
Go away. For this solitude is secure.

(attendants exit left)

A friend you are, but a still greater friend to me is
this army of Achaeans. However, you must explain
why the successful man must provide protection to
his unsuccessful friends. Thus I am prepared.   985

HECUBA
First tell me about my son whom you keep in your house,
Polydorus, from my own hand and from his father's,
whether he still lives. The rest I'll say second.

POLYMESTOR
Sure! Your part in him prospers.[122]

---

121 *Aidôs.* An almost intranslatable word and a concept central to Greek
culture. See Cairns (1993), who studies in great detail the history of
this complex concept, which embraces respect, reverence, a concern
for proper conduct and status. It is fundamentally related to the other
terms of reciprocity such as gratitude and honor that drive the ethical
dynamics of this tragedy.

122 It is important to keep in mind the appearance of the acting area, for
Polydorus' covered corpse is a few feet away from Polymestor while
the Thracian king proves himself a liar in these lines.

HECUBA

Oh my dearest man, how you speak in a way worthy of
  yourself!   990

POLYMESTOR

What second matter do you wish to learn from me?

HECUBA

Does he still remember me at all, his dear mother here?

POLYMESTOR

And in fact he was seeking to approach you here in secret.

HECUBA

And the gold's safe which he bought from Troy?

POLYMESTOR

Safe and guarded in my house!   995

HECUBA

Keep it safe now, and don't covet your neighbors' things.

POLYMESTOR

No way! May I benefit from what is here already, lady!

HECUBA

So do you know what I wish to tell you and your sons?

POLYMESTOR

No, I do not. In your speech you will signal this.

HECUBA

There is, you man dear to me then and so dear to me now... 1000

POLYMESTOR

What matter must both I and my children know?

HECUBA

The gold of Priam's sons, its ancient hiding places deep in the
  earth.

POLYMESTOR

This is what you want to show your son?

HECUBA

Indeed! Through you, of course. For you are a pious man.

POLYMESTOR

Why then do you need presence of my children here?   1005

HECUBA

It's better, in case you should die, that these ones know.

POLYMESTOR
You've spoken well. And it's also wiser thus.

HECUBA
So do you know where are the chambers of Trojan Athena?

POLYMESTOR
The gold is in that place? What sign is there?

HECUBA
A black rock rising above the earth.   1010

POLYMESTOR
So is there anything else of what's there you wish to tell me?

HECUBA
I wish you to keep safe the money with which I came here.

POLYMESTOR
Where is it then? Do you keep it in your robes or have you
    hidden it?

HECUBA
It is kept safe in a mass of plunder inside these chambers.

POLYMESTOR
But where? You're surrounded like a harbor by
    Achaeans here.   1015

HECUBA
The chambers of the spear-won women are private.

POLYMESTOR
And it's safe inside and empty of men?[123]

HECUBA
None of the Achaeans are inside, but we women are alone.
But come into our house; for in fact the Argives long
to free their ships' footing from Troy towards home.   1020
Thus having accomplished all you needed you may return
with your sons to where you lodged my child.[124]

Polymestor and sons enter the skênê, *followed by Hecuba. The Chorus is
left alone.*

---

123 Hecuba is careful to show that Polymestor does not wish to share the
    gold with Agamemnon, as he tries to claim in the trial scene.

124 Clearly this is language that is ominous for the audience, yet it continues
    to raise the expectation, begun at 1006, that Hecuba will kill, not blind,
    Polymestor.

CHORUS

Not yet have you paid, but perhaps you *will* pay justice;
as someone having plunged into a harborless sewer[125]   1025
you will fall away from your heart's desire,
your life lost. For where liability
concurs with Justice and gods there is
a deadly deadly trouble.   1030
The hope of this path will trick you and has driven you
to deadly Hades, you miserable man;
and you'll leave life by a hand unaccustomed to war.[126]

POLYMESTOR *(within)*

Omoi, I'm blinded at the light of my eyes, wretch![127]   1035

CHORUS LEADER[128]

Did you hear the Thracian man's lament, friends?

POLYMESTOR

I cry *omoi* again even more, children, at your miserable slaughter!

CHORUS LEADER

Friends! New troubles are accomplished inside the house.

POLYMESTOR

But may you not escape by a nimble foot;
for I'll strike and crash open the heart of this house.   1040
Look, a blow is readied by a heavy hand.

CHORUS LEADER (*shouting in to Hecuba*)

Do you want us to attack? How it's high time

---

125 Literally, the English word "sewer" here is used as an equivalent for a
Greek term for "bilge," a word with little import for us. But the bilge is,
essentially, the ship's sewer.

126 These lyrics divide the act into two parts and their vicious determination
for vengeance, contrasted with Hecuba's mild surface demeanor, leaves
little doubt that Polymestor will experience some catastrophe. But note
that even the Chorus still expects Polymestor's death, an expectation
denied immediately in the following line.
    The adjective *apolemos* ("unaccustomed to war") in 1034 is used elsewhere
by Euripides (*Ion* 217) to describe the hands of the Bacchants which hold
the deadly wands of Dionysus (*thyrsoi*); this might thus connect to the
designation of the Chorus as "the Bacchants of Hades" below at 1077.

127 Shouts from within the *skênê* also occur early in Sophocles' *Ajax*,
Euripides' *Medea* and Aeschylus' *Agamemnon* 1343-46, a scene to which
this one possibly alludes.

128 At such moments the leader of the Chorus often steps out of the collective and addresses the named characters as an individual.

for our presence as allies for Hecuba and the Trojan women!

Hecuba emerges from the skênê.

HECUBA

Go on and smash, spare nothing, break open the gates;
For never will you set bright sight in your eyes,
nor will you see alive your sons whom I killed.   1045

CHORUS LEADER

So have you laid low the Thracian guest-friend, and do you rule
 him,
my lady, and have you actually done such things as you claim?

HECUBA

You will see him very soon before the house,
blind, moving by blind feet,   1050
and the bodies of his two boys, whom I killed
with these best Trojan women; to me has he paid
justice. And here he comes, as you see, from the house.
But I'll get out of the way and stand back from
the roiling, unconquerable, Thracian rage.   1055

POLYMESTOR *(enters crawling from the* skênê. *The actor now wears
a mask reddened to represent the blood from his eyes. At his entrance the*
ekkyklêma *is wheeled out to display the corpses of his sons.*[129] *)*

Omoi I, where should I go?
where stand, where find harbor?
walking like a four-footed mountain beast
on hand and foot? What sort of path
shall I take, this one or that,   1060
desiring to seize the man-murdering[130] women of Ilium,
the ones who destroyed me?

---

129 The *ekkyklêma* was a wheeled cart (literally it means "the rolled out thing")
that was used to display, sometimes, the imagined interior behind the
skênê or, at other times, the bodies of people killed off-stage. It enables
the playwright to expand quickly the visual world of his action.
Here it would have been impossible for the Athenian audience not to
think of the emergence of the newly blinded Oedipus of Sophocles here,
for the *Oedipus Tyrannos* likely would have been produced only one to
three years before the *Hecuba*. Agamemnon refers to the presence of the
corpses at 1118.

130 The audience would likely have been startled to hear one of Hector's
main epithets in the *Iliad*, one also used to describe Achilles' hands after
they have killed Hector (24.479), designating the Trojan women.

cruel cruel daughters of the Phrygians,
in what corners do they cower in flight from me?   1065

If only you, Helios,[131] might heal, heal
the blinded bloody sockets of my eyes,
exchanging them for light.
Ah, ah —
Silence! I detect the secret step   1070
here of women.[132] Where could I rush at them,
and sate myself with their flesh and bones,
setting out a feast fit for savage beasts,
reaping outrage in
retribution for my atrocity? Oh wretch,   1075
where, how am I carried, leaving my children alone
for the Bacchants of Hades[133] to carve up,
slaughtered, a bloody banquet for dogs,
mercilessly hurled out on the mountainside?
Where can I stand, where sit? where walk?[134]   1080
as a ship with its ropes set at sea,

---

131 The sun god.
132 This signals that the Chorus and Hecuba must be moving around
     Polymestor at this point, perhaps mocking him.
133 "The Bacchants of Hades" is an extraordinary image. The female follow-
     ers of Dionysus are imagined as living in ecstatic joy with their master
     (think of the Messenger's description in the *Bacchae* 677-727), but also
     capable of actions of tremendous, frenzied violence (think of the next
     lines of the *Bacchae* when they attack the shepherds and then a cow, and,
     later, when they tear apart Pentheus with their bare hands); hence their
     connection with death and destruction. Euripides uses this image again
     in the *Heracles* when Amphitryon calls his son a "Bacchant of Hades"
     (1119) in reference to the state Heracles was in when he killed his wife
     and children. Close by (1086, 1122) there are two other references to his
     murders as done while acting as a Bacchant. Froma Zeitlin studies the
     Bacchic imagery in the essay on the *Hecuba* in her 1996 book.
134 Throughout this monody Polymestor's references to his difficult move-
     ment and his rapid-fire, brief, repeated series of questions echo and
     mirror Hecuba's anguished laments about her fears for Polydorus in
     her entrance song (63) and monody after the Chorus informs her of the
     decision to sacrifice Polyxena (154-64). These echoes and Polymestor's
     position on the ground reinforce the sense that Hecuba has fulfilled
     the structure of revenge that turns its new victim into a copy of the
     avenger.

gathering my saffron-flax robe,[135] driven as a guard
of my children upon this den of death?

CHORUS

Oh wretch, you have done such unbearable troubles;   1085
punishments to you who committed acts terrible and shameful
[has some god given who is heavy on you.]

POLYMESTOR

Aiai, come, clan of Thrace, spear-bearing, armed,
on your fine horses, subjects of Ares.   1090
You Achaeans. — you Atreids — help help, I cry, I help!
Oh come, by the gods come!

Does anyone hear, or will none defend me? Why do you delay?

Women destroyed me, the spear-won women; terribly,
terribly we have suffered.   1095

Oh my outrage.
Where should I turn? Where should I journey?
Flying up to heaven's
high vault,   正在指望 Helios to heal him   1100
where Orion or Sirius[136] flings burning   1生
beams of fire from their eyes, or should wretched I
speed into the dark-skinned ship of Hades?   死   1105

CHORUS

It is understandable, whenever someone suffers troubles stron-
    ger than
bearing, to attempt escape from a wretched life.

AGAMEMNON (*enters from right, with attendants*)

I heard your screams and came; for the child of the mountain
    rock,
Echo, was not silent, but has clattered through the army, 1110
producing an uproar. If we hadn't known
the towers of the Phrygians had fallen by the Greeks' spear,
this crashing here would have provided fear in no small portion.

---

135 Like when a ship gathers in its sails while preparing to enter a harbor,
     so Polymestor pulls in his clothing to increase his mobility.
136 See Apollodorus, *Library* I.4.3 Orion was a giant whom Artemis killed.
     Orion was blinded by his prospective father-in-law Oinopion but healed
     by the rays of the sun god Helios. Dawn (Eos) then fell in love with him.
     Sirius, the Dog Star, was associated with drought and heat during fall.

POLYMESTOR

Oh best of friends, I heard and recognized, Agamemnon,
your voice. Do you see what we suffer?   1115

AGAMEMNON

Uh.
Polymestor, you miserable man, who destroyed you?
Who blinded your eyes, bloodied their pupils,
and who killed these boys here? Surely whoever it was
held a great rage at you and your children.

POLYMESTOR

Hecuba, along with spear-won women,   1120
destroyed me —not just destroyed, but worse still.

AGAMEMNON

What are you saying? (*To Hecuba*) You, *you* did this deed, as he
says?
You had the heart, Hecuba, to do this impossible[137] act of daring?

POLYMESTOR

Omoi, what will you say? Is she somewhere nearby, is she?
Give me some sign, say where she is, so that I can grab her with
my hands,   1125
tear her apart and cover her skin with blood.

AGAMEMNON

You there, what is happening to you?

POLYMESTOR

            By the gods I beg you,
let me aim my furious fist against this woman here.[138]

AGAMEMNON

Control yourself. Expel the barbarian from your heart and
speak, so that having heard both you and this woman
in turn   1130
I may decide justly in return for what you are suffering so.[139]

---

137 *Amêchanon* also conveys a sense of "unhealable."

138 Agamemnon's question, and Polymestor's furious interruption of
Agamemnon's line, indicates that the actor must be moving with great
agitation.

139 This is a trial scene, one that uses the conventions of the Athenian
court system, and the outcome of the debate, given Agamemnon's
earlier vacillations to Hecuba, is very much uncertain. As the plaintiff,
Polymestor speaks first.

POLYMESTOR

I would speak then. There was a certain youngest son of Priam,
Polydorus, a son of Hecuba, whom his father Priam
gave from Troy to me to raise in my house,
since he was suspicious of Troy's fall.   1135
This one I killed; but why I killed him,
listen, how it was done well and with wise forethought.
    I feared lest the boy, left hostile to you,
would raise up Troy and inhabit it again,
and that the Achaeans, having realized one of Priam's sons was
    still living,   1140
would gather another armada against the land of the
    Phrygians,[140]
and then ravage this plain of Thrace
in plunder, and there'd be trouble for the neighbors of the
Trojans, the very one in which now, my lord, we were laboring.
Hecuba recognized the fatal lot of her boy   1145
and led me along by this story: how she'd tell me of
the golden treasures of Priam's clan, hidden in Ilium.
She leads me alone with my children into
the tents, so that nobody else might know these things.
I sit on a couch in the middle, having bent my knee;   1150
many daughters of the Trojans, some from the left,
some from the right, took their seats,
as if by a friend, and they were praising the Edonian[141] hand's
weaving, gazing upon these robes under the light;
others were examining my two Thracian spearshafts   1155
and made me naked of my twin-pronged protection.
And as many mothers as there were, full of admiration,
tossing the children in their hands, passing them hand-to-hand

---

140 In isolation, this could be an effective argument for Agamemnon, as he
had overseen, on similar grounds, the murder of Astyanax, Hector's very
young son, after the fall of Troy. Euripides dramatizes this shattering
event a decade later in *The Trojan Women*.

141 A tribe in western Thrace, connected with Mt Pangaeon which was near
the oracle of Dionysus mentioned by Polymestor later (1267). The Chorus
in Sophocles' *Antigone* (955-65) sings of an Edonian king who angered
Dionysus and was thus imprisoned in a cave by the god. There is thus a
double connection with Dionysus, and with Dionysian violence, in this
simple adjective.

so the children might be far from their father.
And then from gentle speeches (how do you suppose?)   1160
they immediately take blades from somewhere in their
   robes and
stab the boys, and others, like octopuses,[142]
all together grab me, holding my arms
and legs. While desiring to defend my boys,
if I could lift up my face,   1165
they seized my hair, and if I stirred my hands
in my misery I achieved nothing because of the mob of women.
Finally, a woe worse than woe,
they completed their terrible deeds; for my eyes —
they grabbed their brooches — they stab the
wretched poor pupils of my eyes and   1170
bloody them; and then throughout the tents they
ran in flight. And I leapt out,
like an animal pursuing the foul murderous bitch dogs,
tracking them along every wall like a hunter,
striking, smashing. I have suffered such things
in pursuit of your favor[143] and in the actual killing of your
   enemy,   1175
Agamemnon. And so that I may not stretch out my speech too
   long —
if someone of those who lived before spoke badly of women,
or someone who lives now or someone in the future,
I shall speak having already abridged all these matters: 1180
neither sea or earth nurtures a race

---

142 Diggle here had adopted the substitution of *polupodôn* (octopuses) for
polemiôn (enemies) in the manuscripts; Gregory finds the comparison
of Trojan women to octopuses "bizarre." But this is, I submit, a bizarre
scene. Moreover, a surviving fragment of Sophocles' lost *Iphigenia* (frag.
307) support's Diggle's reading. Clytemnestra advises her daughter
Iphigenia, about to be betrothed to Achilles, though falsely through the
machinations of Agamemnon: "Be mindful to change the color of your
true thought to [match] your man, as the octopus [adapts its color] to a
rock." Aside from the comparison based upon a blur or multiple arms,
there seems to be a connection based on the need to disguise one's true
self in order to survive.

143 Again, *kharis*. Polymestor clings to the codes of reciprocity in the
implication that he acted in their mutual interest.

such as this one; and, every time, the one who meets them
understands.

CHORUS

Don't be so bold, nor blame
the entire female race, lumping them in with your troubles.[144]
[For there many of us, some of whom who are called
hateful   1185
while others are naturally among the number of the wicked.]

HECUBA

Agamemnon, for humans it was never necessary
for the tongue to have more power than deeds;
But, if one has done good things, one should have said good
words,
but if his deeds were wicked, then his words be rotten,   1190
and never able to speak well about injustice.
So the experts about these things are clever,
but they are not able to be clever forever,
and they die badly. Nobody has ever escaped.

　　　　Your business is part of my preamble;   1195
but I'll go to this man and I'll answer his arguments,
you who claim to have been doubly lightening the Achaeans'
load
and acting because of Agamemnon when you killed my boy.
But, you most vile of men, first, never would the barbarian race
ever become friends with the Greeks,   1200
nor could it. Currying what sort of favor[145]
were you so eager? To form some alliance in marriage,
or being a kinsman, or holding what cause?
Or were they intending to sail back here and

144　The representation of misogyny in Greek tragedy is complex and needs
　　to be handled with care. On the one hand we see comments like these,
　　which attempt to show men scapegoating females for their own behav-
　　ior. Moreover, openly misogynistic characters such as Hippolytus and
　　Creon are shown destroyed in part because of the consequences of such
　　attitudes, and other plays, such as the *Medea*, seem to go out of their
　　way to tell the woman's side of the story (even if it is still men who are
　　telling it). On the other hand, dramas such as the *Medea* also could be
　　seen as reinforcing those misogynistic stereotypes.

145　*Kharis*. Hecuba throws Polymestor's use of reciprocity right back at him
　　throughout her rebuttal.

hack down your harvest? Whom do you think this will
　　persuade?   1205
The gold, if you want to speak the truth,
killed my boy, and your profit.
　　　　Next explain this: how was it, when Troy
prospered, and the towered wall still surrounded the city,
and Priam lived and Hector's spear flourished,   1210
why then, if you really wanted to do favor for this man,
did you not kill the boy you kept and raised in your house,
or bring him alive to the Argives?
But when our light was put out
and the city signalled by smoke it was under enemies,   1215
you cut down a guest-friend who'd come to your hearth.
　　　　In addition to these arguments now hear how you
　　appear evil.
You should have, if you really were a friend to the Achaeans,
brought the gold which you say was not yours but his to keep
and given it to the men who are needy and   1220
who for a long time have been away from their ancestral land.
But you, not even now, can you bear to release it from
your hand, and keep it under your control at home.
And by protecting my boy as you should have protected him,
safe and sound, you would have a great glory;   1225
For amidst troubles the good become friends
most clear; good deeds keep friends every time.
And if you needed money while he prospered,
my boy would have been a great treasure for you;
But now you don't have that man for your friend,   1230
and both the benefit of the gold and your own boys are gone,
and you did it yourself. But I say to you,
Agamemnon, if you defend this man, you will appear evil;
you will benefit a guest-friend neither pious
nor trustworthy where he should be, nor just.   1235
We will say you rejoice in evil men,
being such a one yourself — but I don't verbally abuse my
　　masters.

CHORUS
Pheu pheu. How good matters always give
to mortals the occasion for good words.

AGAMEMNON

Burdensome it is for me to judge another's troubles,   1240
but still a necessity. For it also brings shame
if I take this matter into my hands and then shove it away.
To my mind, so that you know, you seem to have done a favor
neither to me
nor to the Achaeans by killing a man who was a guest-friend,
but merely so that you could have the gold in your own
home.   1245
You say things advantageous to yourself because you're in
trouble.
So it was easier among you people to kill a guest-friend quickly;
but for us Greeks this thing is shameful.[146] *Barbarian.*
How then, having found you innocent, could I escape reproach?
I would not be able. But, since you dared to do   1250
things not noble, submit also to things not of your liking.

POLYMESTOR

Oimoi. By a woman, it seems, I am beaten by a
slave woman, and I will now have to submit and pay justice to
my inferiors.

AGAMEMNON

But is it not justly, since you did evil?

POLYMESTOR

Oimoi my children here and my eyes, wretch!   1255

HECUBA

You feel pain. Why? Don't you think I feel pain for my boy?

POLYMESTOR

You rejoice in your outrageous treatment of me, you villain?

HECUBA

Must I not rejoice in my vengeance against you?

*(Here Polymestor must shift in tone, since the content of his attacks shifts
markedly.)*

POLYMESTOR

But not too fast, whenever the ocean damp —

---

146 The irony here is that Agamemnon's own father, Atreus, killed his
brother's sons while Thyestes was a guest in his house. And this murder
motivates Aegisthus' role in death of Agamemmnon, which Polymestor
prophecies at the end. Who is the barbarian?

HECUBA

— won't ferry me to the borders of Greece?   1260

POLYMESTOR

— will cover you when you have fallen from the masthead —

HECUBA

— when I've happened upon a violent fall at whose hands?

POLYMESTOR

You yourself will place your foot on the ship's mast.

HECUBA

With wings on my back, or in what sort of way?

POLYMESTOR

A bitch dog you'll become, possessing fiery eyes.[147]   1265

HECUBA

How is it you know of my metamorphosis?

POLYMESTOR

The prophet to the Thracians, Dionysus, said these things.[148]

HECUBA

And he prophesied nothing of your current troubles?

POLYMESTOR

No, for otherwise you would never have taken me thus with deceit.

HECUBA

Dead, or alive here shall I complete my life?[149]   1270

POLYMESTOR

Dead; your tomb shall acquire the name...

HECUBA

Won't you say it is named after my shape?

---

147 There is no evidence of a tradition of such a transfiguration before Euripides. Scholars are divided in their interpretations of this metamorphosis. Does it signify an externalization of her internal savagery, as argue Michelini (1987) 172, Nussbaum (1986) 398, and Segal (1993) 161-62; or is it a punishment, but more symbolic of the fierce maternal loyalties thought to characterize dogs, as argue Kovacs (1987) 109, Mossman (1992)197, and Gregory (1999) xxxiv?

148 The Greek word *mantis* can designate both the human speaker for the deity as well as the god himself.

149 This line is hopelessly corrupt in the manuscripts. See Collard (1991).

POLYMESTOR

The tombstone[150] of a wretched bitch, a signpost for sailors.

HECUBA

Nothing is a concern to me since you, at least, have paid back
justice to me.

POLYMESTOR

And necessity is that your daughter Cassandra die.   1275

HECUBA

I spit it back in your face. I give these for you to keep yourself.

POLYMESTOR

The spouse of this man here, a bitter housewife, will kill her —

HECUBA

May the daughter of Tyndareus not yet be so wild with
madness![151]

POLYMESTOR

— and this man himself, when she raises up the axe.

AGAMEMNON

You there, are you mad, and are you in love with falling into
troubles?   1280

POLYMESTOR

Kill me then, since bloody baths await you in Argos.[152]

AGAMEMNON

Will you not haul him off violently, servants?

POLYMESTOR

Do you feel pain, listening?

AGAMEMNON

                    Will you not restrain his mouth?

POLYMESTOR

Shut it! For my speech is complete.

---

150 Cynossema ("tomb of the dog") is the name of a promontory sticking
out from Thracian Chersonese into the Hellespont. See Gregory (1999)
xxxv-xxxvi.

151 This time the daughter of Tyndareus is Clytemnestra, Helen's sister. I
think it is important for one to retain the ambiguity of *mêpô* as "not yet"
(its more common meaning, instead of "never", as Collard suggests) as
it might hint at the desire in Hecuba for violence to Agamemnon.

152 Clytemnestra and his cousin Aegisthus (her lover) kill Agamemnon
while he lies defenseless in the bath following his homecoming.

AGAMEMNON *(to attendants)*
> Will you not as quick as you can
> expel him somewhere on a deserted island,   1285
> since he mouths in this way with too much boldness?

Agamemon's attendants drag Polymestor off to the left. Polymestor likely fights.

> Hecuba, you, Oh you miserable woman, come here and
> bury the two corpses;[153] and you must draw near
> the tents of your masters, women of Troy, because I see
> these winds here escorting us homewards.   1290
> May we sail well to our fatherland, and may
> we see our affairs well at home, freed of these toils here.[154]

(Agamemnon exits right)

CHORUS LEADER
> Go to the harbors and tents, friends,
> to try on the hardships of our masters.
> For necessity does not bend.   1295

After Agamemnon exits right and the Chorus follows, Hecuba is left alone with the corpses, which are withdrawn with the ekkyklêma. *Hecuba follows and enters the tent in order to prepare her children for burial.*

---

153 The two corpses belong to Polydorus, whose body has remained on stage throughout the trial, and to Polyxena, whom Hecuba will finally now go to bury, an action delayed since the discovery of Polydorus' body. Thus will be fulfilled the initial prophecy of Polydorus' ghost that Hecuba would see two corpses of her children on single day (44-5).

154 Why are the winds suddenly rising? These winds could in fact be the beginnings of the great god-sent storm that will wreck the Achaean fleet (*Odyssey* 4.496-516), killing many of its warriors, forcing Menelaus far to the south, and blowing Agamemnon safely across the Aegean so that his wife can kill him at home.

Interpretive Essay

Euripides' *Hecuba* is, to my mind, the single most disturbing of the surviving Greek tragic dramas. It opens, uniquely, with the ghost of an adolescent male describing the mutilation of his body at the hands of a family friend, and it ends with a blazingly dissonant *fortissimo* of angry emotions, as first two and then three characters violently denounce each other. No other Greek tragedy, not even the *Medea*, goes out of its way to make its audience so uncomfortable from the first line to the last. At the very least it belongs to that rarified category that George Steiner has termed "absolute tragedy," in which "the absolute despair, the nihilism in respect of hope" has been obliterated by the drama's events.[1] Steiner includes in this group the *Hecuba, Bacchae, Trojan Women* and *Antigone*. I believe that *Hecuba* goes even further than these other three in its portrayal of the wreckage of human character and in its utter denial of any form of redemptive suffering. These aspects appeal universally to the emotions of modern audiences, yet they must have been equally shattering to ancient ones, and in no small part because *Hecuba* enacts the violation and perversion of several central codes of Greek ethics. Following my exploration of these terms, I shall discuss the themes of slavery and necessity as they are embodied by the Chorus, as well as exploring the role of the Chorus in Euripides' *Hecuba*.

EURIPIDES' *HECUBA* AND THE CRISIS OF VALUES

Reciprocity was the driving force in much of the Greek value system governing relations between human beings and between humans and gods.[2] Several Greek ethical terms, which are all related and lack simple English equivalents, are key to the moral crisis of the *Hecuba*. The reader meeting these terms for the first time should not feel immediately at sea or panicked at the potential conceptual

---

1 Steiner, "Tragedy Pure and Simple", 538 in Silk (1996).
2 On reciprocity in Greek culture see Seaford (1994), and Gill, Postlethwaite and Seaford (1998).

baggage, since, I submit at the risk of a gross exaggeration, this world of reciprocal relations is not completely alien to certain monuments of American culture, such as the *Godfather* films, which represent a world where "favors" are given and expected in return, as is violence. My own students have seen such similarities. So these Greek ethical terms might not be so completely alien after all. The first is *xenia*, the institution of the guest-host relationship that established alliances across generations between families, after initially guaranteeing the security of both guests and hosts from the first contact among strangers.[3] The second is *aidôs* the sense of recognition, reverence, respect, even shame, towards someone of a particular status or with whom one has a special relationship.[4] Then there is *kharis*, the idea of reciprocal gratitude. Next, suppliancy, *hiketeia*, requires that the person supplicated answer and protect the supplicant.[5] Last, blood sacrifice is an institution of reciprocity between gods and men. Each of these five concepts suffers violation, inversion or perversion during the course of the *Hecuba* and their violation leads directly the most unsettling of all Greek reciprocal actions: vengeance. Let us now examine how each works in the drama.

XENIA

The debasement of the guest-host relationship lies at the heart of the *Hecuba's* plot and in some respects is the easiest Greek concept to understand here. The violation of the *xenia* is prevalent throughout the myths of the Trojan War and Homeric epic. Paris absconds with Helen and much of Menelaus' property while acting as Menelaus' innocent guest in Sparta; Zeus, in his cult guise as protector of the *xenia* authorizes the Trojan War to avenge this criminal act. In Book 6 of the *Iliad* the Trojan ally Glaucus and the Achaean warrior Diomedes decide not to fight when they discover their ancestors were guest-friends, and they renew their alliance with an exchange of armor. From its first book, the *Odyssey* is replete with scenes of guests being entertained by their hosts, or not. The suitors of Penelope, refusing to leave her house until she chooses one of them, are certainly bad guests, but they also manage to be simultaneously bad hosts when they do not welcome the disguised Athena and later abuse Odysseus when he masquerades as an old beggar; the suitors, like the Trojans, die for such crimes. And the cannibalistic Cyclops Polyphemus certainly asks for his blinding when he scorns the Zeus who protects

---

3   M. I. Finley (1979).
4   Cairns (1993).
5   Gould (2001).

guests; on the other hand, Odysseus and his men certainly are not model guests either! "All strangers (*xenoi*) are protected by Zeus," exclaims Nausicaa (6.207-8), the daughter of Odysseus' final hosts before his return to Ithaca. One thus harms the guest at considerable peril to one's own life.

The Thracian king Polymestor virtually guarantees his own destruction when he kills the young Polydorus, sent by his father Priam to Polymestor because of the latter's status as a guest-friend, a *xenos*. The greed of Polymestor for Priam's gold overwhelmed his morality. The text is quite insistent on this point, introducing it early and reminding us of it continually. Polymestor is introduced as the guest-friend (*xenos*) of Priam (7). When Polydorus describes his murderer, it is not by name, but by status: "my father's guest-friend slays me." Hecuba similarly, at her horrid realization of her son's death, immediately identifies the killer not as Polymestor but as (710) "my guest-friend," and immediately then asks (715) "Where is the justice of guest-friends?" When Agamemnon asks Hecuba who killed her son, she again says (774), " The Thracian guest-friend killed him." Begging for Agamemnon's help, Hecuba stresses the particular nature of Polymestor not as a simple murder, but a murder of a guest-friend (789-96). She hammers away at this identification of Polymestor as an impious *xenos* (853, 890, 1096, 1216, 1234) until Agamemnon pronounces his judgment of Polymestor in the same language (1243-5):

> To my mind, so that you know, you seem to have done a favor neither to me
> nor to the Achaeans by killing a man who was a guest-friend,
> but merely so that you could have the gold in your own home.

Polymestor, during the trial scene, attempts to justify the murder as an act of *kharis* to the Greek army. Here at least, one reciprocal relationship holds more moral weight than another. One final irony with this concept is that the name of her other dead child, Polyxena, evokes this very relationship: "she who is the guest-friend of many."

AIDÔS

Such a complex set of ideas and emotions involving inhibition are bound up with *aidôs*: respect, fear, shame, reverence. Euripides, so seemingly preoccupied with human psychology and motivation, is particularly interested in its elusiveness. In the *Hippolytus*, produced only a few years before the *Hecuba*, Phaedra, struggling with her unexpressed passion for her stepson Hippolytus, speculates, enigmatically, that the are two types of *aidôs*, one good, the other bad, as each motivates a different behavior. *Aidôs*, despite its seemingly inwardly-directed nature, is in fact bound up with these other forms of social obligations. Indeed, *aidôs* could be described as the emotion that drives the adherence to the *xenia* and suppliancy codes. Polymestor's failure to respect his duties to Polydorus could be described as a failure of *aidôs*. Polymestor is literally shameless, completely lacking in a concern for how others might view him and his actions in violating some of his society's most basic norms. Blindness is thus an apt punishment both practically and thematically. Gregory notes that a Greek proverb holds that *aidôs* resides in the eyes, and *aidôs* is the very quality Polymestor has shown himself to lack.[6] Moreover, there is a connection between *aidôs* and its specific incarnation in Polymestor, his violation of the *xenia*, which resonates in one of the models for the blinding scene, the Cyclops episode in Homer's *Odyssey*.[7] For her part, Hecuba first begs Odysseus to have *aidôs* for her after recounting his suppliancy of her in Troy, and then, when Polymestor arrives, she claims that *aidôs* prevents her from looking him in the eye. She thus subtly points out the sense of shame that he lacks.

KHARIS

Kharis is almost reciprocity itself, meaning something like favor or gratitude that is felt to be owed to someone. It too is exploited in both parts of the play by those who have no real sense of it. First, Odysseus, summing up his argument that warriors should receive as much visible honor as possible so that they will continue to desire to fight, asserts,"gratitude (*kharis*) lasts a long time." Odysseus seems to suggest that only warriors are worthy of *kharis*, since he has just rejected Hecuba's reminder that he owes her his life. Hecuba, desperate to respond to the death of her children, manipulates this value as she did *aidôs*. In one episode which some critics have seen as marking Hecuba's rapid moral decline, she uses Agamemnon's sexual relationship with her daughter Cassandra to suggest he owes her a "favor" (830). She then tries to win Agamemnon's passive assistance that he not interfere with her actions, closing her argument with the promise that he will not appear to be acting on the basis of *kharis* (874). Polymestor then, in the trial scene, appeals to Agamemnon that he killed Polymestor as a favor (*kharis*) to Agamemnon (1174),

---

6 Gregory (1999) 170.
7 See *Odyssey* 9.269-71 and Cairns (1993) 105-13 on *aidôs* and the concern for guests and guest-friends.

and Hecuba throws his language right back at him (1201). It might be significant that Hecuba's oppressor in the drama's first half and her enemy in its second both sophistically use words central to Greek ethics in order to win arguments against her.

HIKETEIA

Supplication is a ritualized act in which the suppliant abases himself before a more powerful being and requests assistance or protection. It is part of the same structure of reciprocity as *kharis*, *aidôs* and *xenia*. Supplication occurs with an expectation of reciprocity, it requires as sense of *aidôs* in order to be effective, and supplication typically takes place between individuals who are not part of the same group; that is, *xenoi*. Physical contact between the players is fundamentally important, since it guarantees the suppliant's status; once the Nurse lays hold Phaedra in the *Hippolytus*, Phaedra cannot deny her requests. As already observed, there are two central scenes of supplication in the *Hecuba* but important also are a refusal to supplicate and the narration of a past act of supplication.

Hecuba figures in all of these acts of supplication. First, she recalls for Odysseus his supplication of her when he was caught by Helen, while he was spying on Troy. He adopted the full suppliant position, on the ground with his hands on Hecuba's knees (245). Foreshadowing his refusal to honor reciprocally Hecuba's request to spare her daughter, he lied to her about his activities. Hecuba now, with the tables turned, drops to her knees in self-abasement and reaches out to Odysseus (273-75).[8] If Hecuba is in fact touching Odysseus, he must break away either at the beginning or end of his own speech, given Hecuba's subsequent lament about her inefficacy. Polyxena must then present a more formidable suppliant than her mother, or the combined pleas of the mother and daughter would move even the hardened Odysseus, since Polyxena's first words to him describe his attempts to avoid her supplication (342-45). She, however, rejects the very idea of self-abasement, but prefers to reclaim the nobility she had lost when the Greeks enslaved her, which she cannot achieve otherwise. Hecuba last supplicates Agamemnon (750) in order to acquire his assistance in obtaining vengeance against Polymestor. She sinks to her knees and remains there for an extended conversa-

---

8 Gould (2001) 41 says Hecuba's supplication is "figurative" and not enacted. I take her words literally and see an actual supplication which Euripides intended to contrast with Polyxena's refusal to engage in any form of supplication, whether real or figurative. Hecuba does spend much time on the ground in this drama.

tion with Agamemnon; she mentions being on her knees still at 787 and remains there at least until Agamemnon seems to break contact with her at 812. Agamemnon, however, unlike Odysseus, at least acknowledges her suppliancy, yet vacillates between the conflicting imperatives of Polymestor's crimes and Polymestor's relationship with Agamemnon's own army. While Hecuba's suppliancy does not win an active assistance from Agamemnon, it does achieve a passive one, since he leaves her with the knowledge that she is inviting Polymestor to her tents with the intention of doing something to him.

BLOOD SACRIFICE

Just are humans are bound to one another with acts of reciprocity, so too are humans to the gods through the exchange of sacrificial victims. Humans make offerings to the gods, usually in the form of domestic animals, and the gods grant blessings to humans in return.[9] The sacrificers burn part of the animal and cook most of the rest for their own consumption. The sacrifice honors the gods, yet provides its participants with a renewed sense of community and a meal. In Book 1 of Homer's *Iliad*, when Chryses, the Trojan priest of Apollo whose daughter has been taken as a prize for Agamemnon, asks for Apollo's help, he reminds the god of the nice temple he has built for him and the numerous animals he has sacrificed in his honor. Apollo, of course, punishes the Greek army with plague. Later in Book 1, once the Greeks restore Chryses' daughter to him, they perform propitiatory sacrifices to Apollo and consume the results. Sacrifice in the *Hecuba* certainly does not function so cleanly, even beyond the human nature of the victim.

Absent from Homer (save for Sarpedon in *Iliad* Book 16), yet prevalent in Greek tragedy, is another sacrificial institution: hero cult. Greek cities that claimed affiliation with the great heroes of the mythic past worshipped them as semi-divine powers whose local graves could grants blessings and curses, the fertility of the earth and victory in war. We see this most clearly in Sophocles' final tragic drama, *Oedipus at Colonus,* where the grave of Oedipus will grant the city that has welcomed it power in battle over its enemies. Greeks would worship heroes in cult similar to gods, with libations of wine and sacrificial killing of animals, though wine and blood would be poured into the ground over the grave, essentially to give sustenance to the hero's spirit. The emotional power of the apparition of Achilles' ghost and the need to appease it arise from hero cult. Achilles demands

---

9 Burkert (1985) 53-60 provides a brief and clear overview of Greek sacrificial ritual.

honor just like divinities in other Euripidean tragic dramas, such as Dionysus in the *Bacchae* and Aphrodite in the *Hippolytus*. Otherwise, divinity is almost completely absent from Euripides' *Hecuba*, in a sense very reminiscent of its cousin, another tragedy of female vengeance, the *Medea*.

Sacrifice in the *Hecuba* is problematic because it involves a human victim, but also because of the nature of the being demanding it and the distinct lack of clarity in the reasoning for the sacrifice. The sacrifice of Polyxena at the end of the Trojan War is symmetrical with that of Iphigenia before the war and the earlier sacrifice is clearly evoked in Euripides' drama. The comparison is instructive. In Aeschylus' *Agamemnon* the prophet Calchas interprets the inability of the Greek fleet to depart Aulis, combined with the destruction of a pregnant hare by two eagles, as signaling the displeasure of Artemis, an anger that can only be appeased by the sacrifice of Agamemnon's daughter Iphigenia to the goddess. This event, while effective for enabling the departure of the fleet, causes an immense crisis and precipitates the entire action of the *Oresteia*. In the *Hecuba*, however, it is unclear what, exactly, Achilles demands; there is a public debate over its fulfillment, and the sacrifice does not seem to achieve the desired outcome, as the winds refuse to turn favorable after the sacrifice.

The ghost of Achilles, like his living predecessor in Homer's *Iliad*, makes a demand of a prize gift of honor that has a discordant effect on the Achaean army. His demand is not represented directly, but reported through three different sources, leaving the motivation for the sacrifice questionable. First, the ghost of Polydorus announces to the theater audience Achilles' demands for a prize, and specifies Polyxena as the victim (40-41). Yet Polydorus does not state that Achilles is preventing the ships from leaving Thrace, leaving open the possibility that Achilles has so confused the army that it finds itself unable to leave. Odysseus repeats that Achilles requests Polyxena in particular (305, 389) and also does not connect causally the apparition of Achilles with any restraining winds. Hecuba's version of the apparition is that the prize should be "some one of the many-troubled Trojan women", yet not necessarily Polyxena. But the Chorus, which narrates at the greatest length the apparition of Achilles, merely quotes a demand for a prize, with no clear idea of its nature (114-15), and then depicts the debate over how best to honor Achilles, whether with blood sacrifice or not. The Chorus seems to imply that the desire to kill Polyxena in sacrifice comes not from Achilles, but from the assembly of the army and Odysseus. Polyxena, as the only available pure virgin typically chosen in Greek myth to appease divine anger, is, to some members of the assembly, the obvious offering. That Achilles' demands are not causing the inability of the fleet to depart is then suggested by Agamemnon's observation that the continuing ill winds after the sacrifice allow Hecuba the time to act against Polymestor. Agamemnon's comment that "god releases no fair breezes" (901) suggests some other force is at work, since "god" (*theos*) cannot denote Achilles and in prior Greek literature heroes lack the power to control weather. Then, his last lines in the drama note that the winds have arrived to take the Greeks home (1290). How has this happened? Why did the sacrifice fail and Hecuba's revenge seemingly work?

The answer, I believe, lies with the crimes committed against Polydorus and his request to the gods for a proper burial. The laws of guest-friendship, sanctified by the gods, are broken, and a human is offered to a hero in sacrifice, against all cultural norms, and, presumably, divine sanction. Polydorus tells that he has been hovering about his mother's tents for as long as she and her captors have been camped in Thrace, a stay prolonged by the appearance of Achilles (30-35). He has asked the gods for burial by his mother, but this cannot happen if the Greeks leave before his body is discovered. The demands of Achilles and the winds are related only in so far as they have some connection with the gods' desire that Polydorus be buried and the crimes of Polymestor be punished. The gods are, in Segal's words, remote and obscure,[10] but they are, in the end, effective. They accept the vengeful punishment of Polymestor almost as an offering to them, a form of sacrifice.[11] Hecuba thus restores the codes of reciprocity among men and between men and gods.

Yet there is little comforting about this restoration, as it comes with a terrible cost to all concerned with the action. Polyxena's beautiful, noble death provides her with escape from the hated life of slavery, yet it need not have happened at all. Hecuba has now matched her antagonist's brutality. The stylized trial debate over her revenge takes place with the bodies of three murdered children in full view of the audience, with a fourth never out of anyone's mind for long. The drama's ending itself disintegrates into a barrage of angry yelling, prophecies of murder and metamorphosis, and an order to abandon the bloody, blinded murderer on an island. Hecuba, depicted as miserable especially in terms of her lost innocent children, has killed two more, and now she will change into a dog with fiery eyes, a transformation that either suggests her fierce maternal loyalties, or, as

---

10 Segal (1993) 219.
11 Mitchell-Boyask (1993).

I believe, externalizes her inner savagery. No commands to establish new rituals are made, as they so often are at the end of Euripidean tragedies, and so there is no hope of order emerging from this chaos. The final words from an actor are spoken by a character the audience knows will die soon himself once the winds he sees rising carry him home. Indeed the winds themselves are of little comfort, since they are, as the audience likely realized, the harbingers of the god-sent storm that will almost completely destroy the Greek fleet as it attempts to leave the area. The Chorus exits with the concluding observations that they must accept their position as servants in their masters' tents and ships because of harsh necessity, *anankê*. So many Greek tragedies end with what often sounds to us like pithy, trite observations about the many shapes of the gods, or how the gods provide unexpected outcomes to events. Here we find only bleak necessity as the driving force of human existence. Humans have enacted this sequence of events, but with little help or prompting by the gods, who are very remote indeed, and who remain, literally, outside of human consideration at the tragedy's close. Euripides *Hecuba* simply projects nothing positive or constructive into the future.

But what has been projected into the future for the characters has been prophesied by Dionysus, whose theater the original audience of the drama is occupying while they hear Polymestor reply to the astonished, furious Hecuba when she asks him how he knows her future (1287): "The prophet to the Thracians, Dionysus, said these things." The god of theater is the prophet of violence and the metamorphosis of humans into beasts. Earlier (1076), the enraged, blinded Polymestor had similarly linked to Dionysus the murderous female slaves who had helped Hecuba, calling them "the Bacchants of Hades," whom, he believes, would "carve up" his sons, presumably for some kind of horrific feast. This association of Dionysus with metamorphosis, with pedicidal fury and the violation of the most sacred human customs, all in the name of justice, points forward to Euripides' culminating vision roughly fifteen years later in the *Bacchae*. The gods are remote, but they have names. They act mysteriously, and the relation of their power to justice in the lives of the humans in this story is as questioned and contested as is that same relationship in the lives of the humans in Athens who watched this drama in the Theater of Dionysus sometime during the 420s, as the moral chaos of the Peloponnesian War grew in intensity.

THE CHORUS AND THE THEMES
OF EURIPIDES' *HECUBA*

The Chorus of Trojan slave women exits the orchestra evoking the power of Necessity, a moment which by itself sums up many of the major themes of Euripides' *Hecuba*. The Chorus throughout this drama serves as a sounding board and focal point for the meaning of the actions articulated by the main characters. This group consists of women of a mix of ages and backgrounds, as typified by the speaking characters of the former Queen Hecuba and the loyal serving woman who presumably had been with her before the sack of Troy. They share their vivid memories of Troy's destruction and their new status as slaves. The protagonist of the drama, unusually, shares the status of the chorus members: a slave, neither higher nor lower, she is like them. Let us now examine the chorus first and then its integration with the drama's main themes.

While the chorus is the one absolutely indispensable part of Greek drama (despite the neglect of it in Aristotle's *Poetics*), it has also been the most difficult to assess properly and thus numerous, and persistent, misunderstandings have arisen over the years.[12] A playwright's participation in the festival of the City Dionysia was completely predicated on his being "granted a chorus" by Athens. The City Dionysia itself can be seen as a choral festival, since, in addition to the dramatic productions, there were choral competitions of dithyrambs (songs in honor of Dionysus), involving dozens of "teams", some of men and others of boys, organized according to deme affiliations which reached across the entire city of Athens. Virtually everybody in the theater audience would have participated in these competitions themselves or had a relative who had done so; the theatrical chorus thus played to an audience of experts. In the theater the chorus dominated each play visually, for it almost never left the orchestra once it entered and their costumes and dancing must have been spectacular, and aurally, for its lyric songs contrasted strongly with the spoken meters of the actors and provided emotional contexts for the experiences of the characters. The chorus, however, was *not* necessarily the vehicle for the poet to express "what he really thought," since the chorus' words were so often driven by the exigencies of the situation. Nor was the chorus, while it

---

12 Three particularly valuable recent essays that focus on the chorus and its role are "A Show for Dionysus" and "Form and Performance," both by P.E. Easterling (36-53 in Easterling 1997) and John Gould, "Tragedy and the Collective Experience" (217-43 in Silk 1996). For a general treatment of the chorus and the ancient evidence for it, see Csapo and Slater (1995) 349-68.

frequently served as a communal foil against the heroic egoism of the characters embodied by the actors, necessarily representative of the civic collective of the city of Athens, simply because its identity could be foreign, slave, female, and sometimes all three combined. While the chorus can be the vehicle for more extended meditations on the meaning of the drama's events, it must be considered a character in the drama. Chorus members express fears, hopes, joy and sadness. A chorus can be confused; indeed, to some a chorus can seem stupid at these moments of confusion (and one might productively compare here the frequent bewilderment of Jesus' disciples in the Gospels). In other words, a dramatist's use of a chorus will shift as the needs of a situation require, so it is better to restrict discussion of the function of the chorus to broad parameters. I thus offer two. First the chorus serves as a sounding board for the events that have occurred in the scene before an ode, offering some initial guidance for the audience to think about those events, even if the initial focus is confusion or terror. The thoughts of the chorus can also prepare the audience for the next scene by considering the possible sequence of events that might ensue; such preparation can involve misdirection by the poet, wherein the chorus establishes an expectation that is frustrated. The chorus thus helps shape the action into the broader parameters of human experience and understanding. Second, the chorus can be agents in that action. Such function ranges from a chorus that conspires with the protagonist but has no physical part, as in the case of the Corinthian Women in Euripides' *Medea* or the Sailors in Sophocles' *Philoctetes*, to a chorus that not only participates, but hounds the protagonist across the stage, as with the Furies in the *Eumenides* of Aeschylus. In some sense, the best ways for us to view the chorus is, first, that the dramatist used it according the particular needs of the individual drama and that this function could shift inside the drama depending on the given situation. Second, the choral voice contrasts with the named heroes on stage and, in the words of John Gould (222), "articulates a collective 'anonymous' experience and response to events. The central, heroic characters of the tragic action struggle to maintain and enforce an individual identity and authority and to impose meaning on the flux events in terms of that identity, the individual 'I'." These comments are broad, yet effectively describe a very diverse range of tragic dramas, from the *Oedipus Tyrannus* to the *Hecuba*.

The Chorus of Euripides' *Hecuba* is typically Euripidean in its identity, since Euripides frequently makes his chorus female, barbarian or slaves (here all three!) but slightly less typical in its organic relationship to the action. Over the centuries, critics, beginning with

Aristotle in the *Poetics*, have faulted Euripides' handling of the chorus for being insufficiently connected to its drama's action, but, while such charges are, I believe, overblown and based on unsympathetic readings, the *Hecuba* is certainly one drama that directly refutes them. Its protagonist is "one of them", and they not only commiserate with her, but also conspire with her and assist in her vengeance against Polymestor. Their songs clearly are meditations, often quite moving ones, on their experiences and they are deeply engaged with the events of the drama; like Hecuba, they were once free and now are slaves. They shared the nightmare of Troy's destruction. Gould further comments on the particularly Euripidean nature of choruses that are so frequently women, foreign and captives of war in dramas that are dominated by female protagonists:

> . . . Euripides simultaneously creates a further perspective, in those plays which place a woman at the centre of the tragic action (and they are a majority of his plays), by setting up a single axis of dramatic tension which aligns, rather than confronts, female protagonist with female chorus and thus enforces a point of view from which the 'heroic' world of men is thus seen as wholly alien: sometimes frighteningly and violently destructive, sometimes distant and incomprehensible, sometimes despicable and without honour.

Gould's general assessment of Euripidean choruses and their place in the larger dramas fits the *Hecuba* to a tee, for it thus captures the ability of the women to "stay on message" in the face of different heroic male worlds of first Achilles (violently destructive and terrifying) and then Odysseus (without honor) and Polymestor (despicable).

These demands of this male world are so totalizing that they receive the title of Necessity in Euripides' *Hecuba*, and this concept becomes one of the major themes of this drama.[13] In my translation, forms of "necessary" and "necessity" occur fifteen times (and "compel" or "compulsion" another seven), covering a wide range of situations, and almost invariably at crucial moments in the action. Hecuba asks, in response to the news of Polyxena's impending death, "Was it that **necessity** compelled them to human sacrifice" (260); the question itself implies its own answer. Polyxena's resignation to the act, "Thus shall I submit both for the sake of **necessity**, and because I desire death." (346-47)," suggests a more contingent form of necessity, an attitude Hecuba

---

13 See Arrowsmith's brief but powerful discussion of this theme, (1959) 490-92.

then picks up in her plea to Odysseus to kill her alongside Polyxena: "There is great **necessity** for me to die with my daughter" (396). Later (1237) the Chorus laments how "the laws of **necessity**" radically alters friendships and enmities among men, and the raging blinded Polymestor prophecies to Hecuba "**necessity** is that your daughter Cassandra die" (1275). The Chorus then closes the drama with the observation (1295) "**necessity** does not bend." Those last two instances point towards a more traditional Greek conception of Necessity as part of Moira, the Greek word that most closely approximates our notion of fate, but, for the most part, necessity in the Hecuba seems frequently more a projection of the inner desires of a character, or a pretext used to cover more undesirable actions—political, not moral or cosmic necessity. It seems also to be used to connote the recognition of the harsher realities of human suffering in a world increasingly dominated by power politics or the acknowledgement of an almost Aristotelean inevitability of events once certain actions occur, given human nature. In both of these senses, what is necessary is really what one must accept out of the weakness of one's position. Thus, the Chorus, remembering the events of a decade previously, realizes that pain and disaster became "necessary" as soon as Paris began cutting the wood to make the ship to sail after Helen (629-33). Yet, Necessity, as an impersonal structure of the universe, is closely allied with *Tuchê*, best translated as "Fortune" or "Luck," and Hecuba herself articulates the belief that nobody's *Tuchê* lasts forever, and the rulers will eventually become the ruled, the killers the killed.

Hecuba and her comrades have lived that recognition, having endured slavery, and slavery is our next subject. The primal scene of Greek myth is the destruction of a city, Troy, which functions like the loss of the Garden of Eden in the Greek mythic consciousness, and perhaps the most overwhelming horror, I would suggest, in the literary incarnations of the fall of Troy is what happens to its victims; not to the dead, but to the living. This fear is especially true during the years of the Peloponnesian War, when Greece saw cities annihilated, their men killed and their women taken away into slavery. Sitting in the Theater of Dionysus, watching Euripides' *Hecuba*, would have been men who had several years before debated the destruction of the entire population of Mytilene on the island of Lesbos, voting first to condemn all and the next day a reversal, with only those guilty of active rebellion sentenced to death. Roughly a decade later, these men would decide to kill all of the grown men of Melos, enslaving the women and children, because the Melians refused to become part of the Athenian empire. The experience of watching other men act the part of female slaves after their city is ruined in war was not simply an aesthetic one for this audience, since the treatment of prisoners of war surely was an issue being debated with regularity in Athens. The reality of the loss of freedom is depicted with great regularity in Greek drama, from Aeschylus' *Suppliant Women* through the late dramas of Euripides. It is thus important for a modern American reader to keep in mind that slavery in classical Greece differed from American slavery before the Civil War in being based on the success (or lack thereof) in war and not on skin color. Defeat in battle meant death or slavery, and, thus for the Greeks there was a fate worse than death: slavery. While some slaves served as tutors for children in prosperous families, many others suffered terribly laboring in the silver mines which Athens owned and which helped finance the wars in which these human beings might became slaves. The slaves in Euripides' *Hecuba* and Hecuba herself lament that they did not die at the sack of Troy. Polyxena sees her own death as a form of liberation from her slavery. The sociologist Orlando Patterson has seen in the slave choruses of Greek tragedy, especially in those of Euripides, an expression of "a powerful drive for personal freedom"[14] that represented the deep preoccupation in Athenian thought with liberty. In the funeral oration of Pericles which Thucydides preserves in his *History of the Peloponnesian War*, Pericles regularly circles back to the fundamental concept and reality of freedom that drive the conduct of their struggle against Sparta. In Pericles' speech, Patterson observes, "personal freedom is here defined in terms of an antithesis to slavery."[15] Thus, to an Athenian watching Euripides' *Hecuba*, the experiences of Hecuba, Polyxena and the Chorus of Trojan women represent his deepest fears. Slavery, and the fear of it, drives the drama's themes and imagery; the constant references to light and dark, to eyes and blindness, are metaphors for freedom and slavery. We see this expressed with particular power in Polyxena and Polymestor. As Polyxena expresses her desire to die she proclaims, "From free eyes I release this light" (366-67)" and then, further preparing for death, "now I shall behold the sun's final ray and circle," and even her final lines evoke her departure from the sun of the living (435). The metaphorical complement to Polyxena's free eyes is the blinding of Polymestor, since, set in such a context, "the gouging out of eyes, then, must mean the destruction of a person's freedom."[16] Euripides

---

14 Patterson (1991) 110. See in general Chapter 7, "A Woman's Song", for a discussion of slavery in Greek tragedy.

15 Patterson (1991) 101.

16 Patterson (1991) 118.

underscores Hecuba's approximation of Polymestor to her condition by presenting him, after the blinding, moving like her in her first appearance, singing like her in some of the same disconnected, frantic speech patterns. Once he loses the trial to her, his horror is that he has been beaten by and is thus now lower than a slave woman.

And yet, this tragedy forces its audience to ask who are the real slaves? Polyxena dies in utter freedom, in control of the circumstances of her own death. The king Polymestor, as we have already seen, becomes like a slave in the control greed has over his actions, a condition his blindness then makes physically manifest. Odysseus and Agamemnon seem slaves to the opinion of others. Indeed, it is the latter's reluctance to help Hecuba out of concerns over appearance to assert openly (864): " There is nobody among mortals who is free." Euripides seems to be suggesting that inner freedom is the more meaningful form of liberty.

With the nature of the chorus in general and these two themes of necessity and slavery established, let us see how the choral songs in Euripides' *Hecuba* reflect on and interact with the drama as a whole. The songs are all outlined in the structural synopsis located earlier in this volume, just before the translation. In general one might say that the primary impetus of these songs, as in so many Greek tragedies, is for the Chorus to make sense, both for itself and the audience, of what is happening. For answers, the Chorus looks first to the future, then to the past, and finally to the distant past.

444-83 First Choral Song: Polyxena has thus expressed her desire to escape slavery through a noble, willing death on the sacrificial altar, which prompts the Chorus to wonder about its own future. They know they will be slaves, but, despite that generally unwelcome reality, they know that a slave's life can vary widely in its level of hardship, so they hope for the best, and they thus speculate at their possible destinations, first speculating about Greece in general, then Delos and then Athens itself. The insertion of Athens here, as with the language of the Athenian Assembly and the mention of the sons of the Athenian hero Theseus in the debate over the sacrifice of Polyxena, moves the world of the Trojan War closer to the world of the theater audience than anything even implied in Homer. Even Delos, one of the two main shrines to Apollo, has contemporary significance, because the Chorus wonders whether it might participate in the Dance of the Maidens at the Delian Festival of Apollo, which may have just recently been restored by the Athenians (Thucydides 3.104). But such festival dances were more the venue for free women, not slaves, a cold reality that is set against their similarly false hopes for life in Athens in the succeeding *strophe*, where the Chorus entertains the fantasy that it might help embroider the robe to be presented to the goddess Athena at the Panathenaic Festival, another anachronism designed to bridge the mythical world of the action and the contemporary world of the audience. Again, these hopes are delusion. Polyxena's fine words have inspired the Chorus to dream, yet such dreams last only a moment, and the chorus members seems to awaken suddenly, in the closing *antistrophe*, from their reverie to face anew that their home is gone and they are now slaves. Their lament, "I in a foreign land am called slave," echoes Polyxena from the previous scene where first in her list of reasons to prefer a noble death over a wretched life is the very title of "slave:" "But now I am a slave. First, the very name, unaccustomed, makes me love death" (357-58). They then see Talthybius enter with his report of the death of Polyxena.

629-57 Second Choral Song: That sacrificial narrative, followed by Hecuba's lamentful recognition that human achievements and happiness are only ephemeral, unstable vanities, prompts the Chorus to surrender its earlier concerns for the future and instead to probe the past for an understanding of their suffering, with the first of two songs specifically on the fall of Troy; this is the briefest of the three songs, a relatively quick interlude between the impact of the two separate deaths of her children on Hecuba. Their remembrance of Paris' departure to win Helen is filled with the language of necessity, compulsion, labor, as if the Chorus, faced with the renewal of suffering in the form of Hecuba's grief over Polyxena, has surrendered itself to the acceptance of their lot as "necessary" and inevitable. The squalor of their new life and the destruction of their marriage beds in the epode contrasts poignantly with Paris' pursuit of "the bed of Helen, whom gold-gleaming Helios illuminates as most beautiful" (635-37). Yet, like the first choral song, the second closes with an even more extraordinary bridge between suffering ancient and modern, with its evocation of two grieving women in Sparta: one, a young bride weeping, presumably at the news of her husband's death, and the other an old woman shredding her face with her fingernails in agony over her lost children. There were many cities cooperating in the mythical war at Troy, so the poet's choice of Sparta here surely has contemporary urgency for the real Peloponnesian War, especially with the anachronistic references in the first choral song. Euripides sets before his audience a Hecuba-like figure in the city of the audience's enemy, grieving like the figure in whom the audience has just invested a tremendous amount of highly emotional sympathy. This is the detritus of war, which here lacks a noble purpose and heroic vision.

Again, there is no redemptive suffering here. Yet this sense of the humanity of one's enemy is not new in Greek literature, for Homer's epic takes great pains to depict the Trojans as full human beings with the same dreams and nightmares as the Greeks, most notably in the engagement of Priam and Achilles in the last book of the *Iliad*.

905-51 Third Choral Song: The Chorus moves back to the past again here, but with a more individualized reminiscence of Troy's fall. Instead of linking the mythical past with the present as in the previous two songs, Euripides dwells on a transient moment of domestic happiness, and its loss, that are recognizable by any human being. The women of the Chorus present a distinctly feminine version of that night, dwelling on their last evening with their husbands in false joy over the departure of the Greek armada. Marriage, after emerging in the previous song as a theme, becomes the prominent theme in this ode, contrasting the lost marriages of the Trojans with the happiness of Paris and Helen for the past decade. The husband and wife here further suggest the denial of adult life to Polydorus and Polyxena, dead before they even have a chance to lose their married happiness. In the epode the Chorus expresses their sorrow over losing their identities first as wives and then as Trojans, all because of Helen and Paris, whom they close the song by cursing. The verbal violence of this curse signals their transformation, mirroring Hecuba, from passive sufferer to active avenger.

Here the songs cease, the Chorus stops dancing, and it becomes an accomplice to the deception of Polymestor, taunting him after he exits into Hecuba's tents in pursuit of gold and exulting in the screams of pain they hear from him within. The Chorus produces a few couplets to provide transitions between the speeches of the main characters, but it seems to lose its capacity to frame and to contextualize the action as it becomes part of it. Polymestor takes over the normal laments that we see late in tragedies, but nobody joins in with him in his solo songs, because nobody can sympathize with him and thus participate in his grief. His is the most solo of monodies imaginable. The slaves have won. They are triumphant. After Agamemnon decides the trial in favor of Hecuba, Polymestor's raging grief turns immediately to disgust that he was beaten by "a slave woman" (1252-53). Yet the triumph is short-lived, as Agamemnon sees it is now possible to depart and orders the ships ready. The Chorus now must face the permanence of their new lives as slaves. Thus they finally concede to that great principle (god?) Necessity, for "Necessity does not bend."[17]

---

17 The adjective *sterros* here, meaning "inflexible, rigid," echoes line 296 here it is applied to human nature (*sterros anthrôpou phusis*).

Bibliography and Works Cited

GENERAL WORKS ON GREEK CULTURE

Adkins, A. W. H. *Merit and Responsibility: A Study in Greek Values.* (Oxford, 1960)

Blundell, S. *Women in Ancient Greece.* (Cambridge, Mass., 1995)

Burkert, W. *Homo Necans: The Anthropology of Ancient Greek Sacrificial Ritual and Myth.* tr. Bing. (Berkeley, 1983)

————. *Greek Religion.* tr. Raffan. (Cambridge, Mass, 1985)

Cairns, D. *Aidôs: The Psychology of Honour and Shame in Ancient Greek Literature.* (Oxford, 1993)

Dodds, E. R. *The Greeks and the Irrational* (Berkeley, 1951)

Finley. M. I. *The World of Odysseus.* 2nd rev. ed. (Harmondsworth, 1979)

Gill, C. N. Postlethwaite, and R. Seaford, eds. *Reciprocity in Ancient Greece,* eds. (1998)

Gould, J. *Myth, Ritual Memory and Exchange.* (Oxford, 2001)

Guthrie, W. K. C. *The Sophists.* (Cambridge, l991)

MacDowell, D. *The Law in Classical Athens.* (Ithaca, 1978)

Oakley, J. and R. Sinos. *The Wedding in Ancient Athens* (Madison, 1993)

Parker, R. *Athenian Religion: A History.* (Oxford, 1996)

Patterson, O. *Freedom in the Making of Western Culture.* (New York, 1991)

Pomeroy, S. et al. *Ancient Greece: A Political, Social and Cultural History* (Oxford 1999)

Seaford, R. *Reciprocity and Ritual. Homer and Tragedy in the Developing City-State.* (Oxford, 1994)

Williams, B. *Shame and Necessity* (Berkeley and Los Angeles, 1993)

The World of Athens: An Introduction to Classical Athenian Culture. Joint Association of Classical Teachers (Cambridge, UK, 1984)

GENERAL WORKS ON GREEK TRAGEDY

Arrowsmith, W. "The Criticism of Greek Tragedy." *Tulane Drama Review* 3 (1959): 31-57.

————. "A Greek Theater of Ideas" *Arion* 2 no. 3 (1963): 32-56.

Burnett, A. *Revenge in Attic and Later Tragedy.* Sather Classical Lectures 62. (Berkeley, 1998)

Buxton, R. G. A. *Persuasion in Greek Tragedy: A Study of Peitho.* (Cambridge, UK, 1982)

Connor, W.R. "City Dionysia and Athenian Democracy," *Class. et Med.* 40 (1989) 7-32 - - - . "Civil Society, Dionysiac Festival, and the Athenian Democracy," 217-26 in *Demokratia: A Conversation on Democracies, Ancient and Modern.* J. Ober and C. Hedrick, eds. (Princeton, 1996)

Csapo, E. and W. Slater. *The Context of Ancient Drama* (Ann Arbor, 1995)

Easterling, P.E. and Bernard Knox, eds. *The Cambridge History of Classical Literature*, vol. 1   (Cambridge, 1985)

Easterling, P.E., ed. *The Cambridge Companion to Greek Tragedy.* (Cambridge, 1997)

Foley, H. 2001. *Female Acts in Greek Tragedy.* (Princeton, 2001)

Golder, H. and S. Scully, eds.. *The Chorus in Greek Tragedy and Culture.* Arion 3.1 (1994-5) and 4.1 (1996).

Goldhill, S. *Reading Greek Tragedy* (Cambridge, 1986)

————. "The Great Dionysia and Civic Ideology." 97-129 in Winkler and Zeitlin.

————. "The Audience of Athenian Tragedy." 54-68 in Easterling, *Cambridge Companion.*

————. "Civic Ideology and the Problem of Difference: The Politics of Aeschylean Tragedy, Once Again," *Journal of Hellenic Studies* 120 (2000) 34-56

Griffin, J. "The Social Function of Attic Tragedy." *Classical Quarterly* 48 (1998): 39-61.

Hall, E. *Inventing the Barbarian.* (Oxford, 1989)

Jones, J. *On Aristotle and Greek Tragedy.* (London, 1962)

Lesky, A. *Greek Tragic Poetry*, tr. M. Dillon. (New Haven, 1983)

Loraux, N. *Tragic Ways of Killing a Woman.* tr. Anthony Forster. (Cambridge, 1987)

Mastronarde, D. "Actors on High: The Skene Roof, the Crane, and the Gods in Attic Drama." *Classical Antiquity* 9 (1990): 247-94.

McClure, L. *Spoken Like a Woman : Speech and Gender in Athenian Drama.* (Princeton, 1999)

Nagy, G. "Transformations of Choral Lyric Traditions in the Context of Athenian State Theater," *Arion* 3 (1995) 41-55.

Nussbaum, M. *The Fragility of Goodness: Luck and Ethics in Greek Tragedy and Philosophy.* (Cambridge, 1986)

Pelling, C., ed. *Greek Tragedy and the Historian*. (Oxford, 1997)

Rehm, R. *Greek Tragic Theatre*. (New York, 1992)

Rhodes , P. J., "Nothing to Do with Democracy: Athenian Drama and the Polis," *Journal of Hellenic Studies* 123 (2003) 104-19

Seaford, R. "The Tragic Wedding." *Journal of Hellenic Studies* 107 (1987) 106-30

————. "The Social Function of Attic Tragedy: A Response to Jasper Griffin." *Classical Quarterly* 50 (2000) 30-44

Segal, C. *Interpreting Greek Tragedy: Myth, Poetry, Text*. (Ithaca, 1986)

Silk, M., ed. *Tragedy and the Tragic: Greek Theatre and Beyond*. (Oxford, 1996)

Taplin, O. *Greek Tragedy in Action*. (Berkeley and Los Angeles, 1978)

Vernant, J.-P. and P. Vidal-Naquet, *Myth and Tragedy in Ancient Greece*, tr. J. Lloyd (New York, 1988)

Wiles, D. *Tragedy in Athens: Performance Space and Theatrical Meaning*. (Cambridge, UK, 1997)

Wilson, P. *The Athenian Institution of the Khoregia: The Chorus, the City, and the Stage* (Cambridge, UK, 2000)

Winkler, J. and F. Zeitlin, eds. *Nothing to Do With Dionysos? Athenian Drama in its Social Context*. (Princeton, 1990)

Zeitlin, F. *Playing the Other: Gender and Society in Classical Greek Literature* (Chicago, 1996.)

GENERAL WORKS ON EURIPIDES

Barlow, S. *The Imagery of Euripides: A Study in the Dramatic Use of Pictorial Language*. 2nd ed. (Bristol, U.K, 1986.)

Burian, Peter, ed. *Directions in Euripidean Criticism*. (Durham,1985)

Burnett, Anne Pippin. *Catastrophe Survived: Euripides' Plays of Mixed Reversal*. (Oxford, 1971)

Collard, C. "Formal Debates in Euripides' Drama." *Greece & Rome*. 2nd ser. 22.1

(1975): 58-71.

————. *Euripides. Greece and Rome. New Series in Classics*, 14. (Oxford, 1981)

Conacher, D.J. *Euripidean Drama: Myth, Theme and Structure*. (Toronto, 1967)

Dunn, F. *Tragedy's End: Closure and Innovation in Euripidean Drama*. (Oxford, 1996)

Finley, J. "Euripides and Thucydides." *Harvard Studies in Classical Philology* 49 (1938) 23-66

Foley, H. *Ritual Irony: Poetry and Sacrifice in Euripides*. (Ithaca, 1985)

Gregory, J. *Euripides and the Instruction of the Athenians*. (Ann Arbor, 1991)

Halleran, M. *The Stagecraft in Euripides*. (London, 1985)

Jong, I. de. *Narrative in Drama: the Art of the Euripidean Messenger-speech.* (Leiden, 1991)

Lloyd, M. *The Agon in Euripides.* (Oxford, 1992)

Michelini, A. *Euripides and the Tragic Tradition.* (Madison, 1987)

Mitchell-Boyask, R., ed. *Approaches to Teaching the Dramas of Euripides* (New York, 2002)

Mossman, J., ed. *Oxford Readings in Classical Studies: Euripides.* (Oxford, 2003)

Rabinowitz, N. *Anxiety Veiled: Euripides and the Traffic in Women.* (Ithaca, 1993)

Scullion, S. "Euripides and Macedon, or the Silence of the Frogs," *Classical Quarterly* 53 (2003) 389-400.

Segal, C. *Euripides and the Poetics of Sorrow. Art, Gender, and Commemoration in Alcestis, Hippolytus, and Hecuba.* (Durham, 1993)

Segal, E. *Euripides: A Collection of Critical Essays.* (Englewood Cliffs, 1968)

Winnington-Ingram, R. P. "Euripides: Poietes Sophos." *Arethusa* 2 (1969): 127-42

WORKS ON EURIPIDES' HECUBA

GREEK EDITIONS WITH COMMENTARY:

Collard, C. *Euripides: Hecuba.* (Warminster, 1991)

Gregory, J. *Euripides: Hecuba.* (Atlanta, 1999)

Arrowsmith, W. Introduction to translation of Euripides' *Hecuba.* 488-93 in *The Complete Greek Tragedies. Volume III: Euripides.* Eds. D. Grene and R. Lattimore (Chicago, 1959)

Burnett, A. P. "Hekabe the Dog." *Arethusa* 27 (1994): 151-64

Gregory, J. "Genealogy and Intertextuality in *Hecuba.*" AJP 116 (1995) 389-97

————. "*Hecuba* and the Political Dimension of Tragedy." 166-77 in Mitchell-Boyask 2002.

Heath, Malcolm, "'Iure principem locum tenet': Euripides' *Hecuba.*" 218-60 in Mossman 2003.

Hogan, J. C. "Thucydides 3.52-68 and Euripides' *Hecuba.*" *Phoenix* 26 (1972): 241-57

Kovacs, D. *The Heroic Muse.* (Baltimore, 1987)

Meridor, R. "Hecuba's Revenge." *American Journal of Philology* 99 (1978): 28-35

Mitchell-Boyask, R. "Sacrifice and Revenge in Euripides' *Hecuba.*" *Ramus* 22 (1993): 116-34

Mossman, J. *Wild Justice: A Study of Euripides'* Hecuba. (Oxford, 1999)

Pantelis, M. "The Dead Hero: Euripides' *Hecuba.*" 58-83 in *Achilles in Greek Tragedy.* (Cambridge, 2002)

Reckford. K. "Concepts of Demoralization in the *Hecuba.*" 112-28 in Burian 1985.

Scodel, Ruth "Domon agalma: Virgin Sacrifice and Aesthetic Object" *Transactions of the American Philological Association* 126 (1996) 111-128

Thalmann, W. "Euripides and Aeschylus." *Classical Antiquity* 12 (1993): 126-59